STITCHERY AND CRAFTS

Better Homes and Gardens
STITCHERY AND CRAFTS

A COMPLETE GUIDE TO THE MOST REWARDING
STITCHERY AND CRAFT PROJECTS
FOR THE WHOLE FAMILY

MEREDITH PRESS   NEW YORK   DES MOINES

CONTENTS

STITCHERY

Beautiful handcrafted items for your home reflect your own interests and taste, are personal treasures you'll cherish and enjoy for years to come. Work with the help of a sewing machine or by hand—either way, distinctive and useful stitchery will give you a sense of real satisfaction.

You can make a traditional rocker the center of interest with a new contemporary cover, left. The hot pinks, purples, oranges, golds, and the reds are appliqued with straight stitches running up and down. If there's a stripe in the fabric you are using, place it vertically so the stitching will lose itself after leaving the appliqued portion. See complete directions given on pages 138, 139.

Print is outlined by stitching, making it stand out from background. A variation of trapunto, stitching holds top, batting, backing together. If you wish, baste the three layers together before you start stitching. Soft fabrics are easiest to work with.

Team techniques of applique and machine stitching to get effect of a modern painting, right. Anyone who can sew a straight seam can "draw" penlike lines to hold applique in place. Garner scraps of felt, burlap, denim, and linen from previous sewing efforts. Thread is same as you use for regular sewing.

Work slowly, steadily. Begin by doodling. Try up and down movement. Designers: H. Silver, Edith Reynolds.

Your sewing machine can whiz through quilts or throws that once took weeks to complete. The fabric squares in the throw shown below measure 4½ inches; the rectangles measure 4½ by 8½ inches. These are zigzag-stitched to the backing of the throw.

Pin arrangement onto backing fabric. Machine baste with a narrow zigzag or chain stitch. Do final sewing with decorative stitch. Trim with binding.

STITCHERY

Trapunto in a hurry! Striped fabric alternates one stuffed line, one flat. Sew one edge of stripe, put cotton cording in, sew second side. Trim with bias tape. For printed pillow, allow more material than needed for top. Sew two-thirds distance around flower; add stuffing without removing fabric from machine. To make pillow, lower left, applique the design to the top using satin stitch on machine.

Favorite designs are captured on pillows, above. For rectangular ones, cut a square piece of fabric using half for front and rest for the back. Pin or baste applique pieces to top. Stitch with solid zigzag on large pieces, narrower width on small ones.

Try this idea if you hesitate to make a quilt because it takes too long. Add originality to a ready-made bedspread with these paper doll beauties. Purchase a floor-length cover to fit your bed. Lay cutout figures at lower edge. Baste first, then sew with satin stitch set at full width. Complete directions are on pages 139 and 140-141.

Hang dolls, repeated in felt, for a clever headboard. Cut four girl figures and two boy figures. With wrong sides together, stitch following seam line on the outer edges. Stuff as you go with shredded foam, kapok, or nylon stockings. Place the two girl figures on each side of boy with arms meeting. Tack arms together. Sew drapery rings on the outside arms of the two girls to hang the pillows on the wall.

A quick and easy way to make a teen-age surprise for that next "platter" party—a tote for carrying a current favorite's record and a matching pillow to sit on.

First, cut out a petal pattern on lightweight cardboard, then trace around it on felt with tailor's chalk. Cut out the petals and pin them in place on circles of felt that contrast in color. Select the decorative stitch on your zigzag machine and let your needle fly in circles. Line bag with plastic. Designs: Jean Ray Laury, Edith Reynolds. How-to directions are given on page 139.

FELT RUGS

Anyone who can thread a needle (either by hand or by machine) can create an area rug made from felt. Jean Ray Laury fashioned these designs, using vivid color combinations as a painter would. Best of all, each rug is easy and inexpensive to make. A heavier felt is preferable for the base color (50 percent wool or more works best). In appliqueing, the separate designs are applied directly to the background. Set machine for full width of satin-stitch and use heavy-duty mercerized threads related in color to the fabric. If appliqueing by hand, use whip stitch or buttonhole stitch. Trim with cotton or wool fringe; fringe overlaps raw edge.

Wide strips, narrow strips, short strips, or long strips of bold colors make an interesting composition when you sew them to a solid felt base, left. Closely related colors work best. Try several arrangements, using variations in width of bands and spaces. When a desired arrangement is found, pin and baste before sewing. To avoid wrinkles, sew in the same direction. Top stitch fringe to the rug to finish it.

Storybook motifs in wake-up colors make rug, right, especially appropriate for children—but grownups will delight in it, too. Designs are cut, then appliqued to a white felt background. Take care not to stretch the felt as you work. Pattern, shown on page 144, contains many motifs you could use on a bedspread, a book cover—or frame and arrange in an attractive grouping of pictures for a nursery wall.

Felt comes in a wide range of dramatic colors that are brilliant, beautiful. The heavy-duty ball fringe that is used to trim rug is available from drapery departments.

For beauty underfoot and durability, add a colorful area rug to a bare floor or fine carpet. The area rug, below, complements the beauty of the parquet floor. To duplicate this rug, combine felt motifs in shades of gold, white, light and dark green with contrasting touches of mandarin orange and red. You can borrow parts of the design to create your own screen, placemat, or wall hanging. The complete pattern for rug is given on pages 142 and 143.

A rubber rug pad or carpet pad can be used under any of these rugs to make them skidproof. Or paint with a liquid which is designed for this purpose. Spray with soil-resistant liquid when finished. Dry clean a rug that's soiled.

Feast your eyes on these long-wearing rugs that you hook yourself. Embellished with sharp, pure colors, these dramatic designs are suitable for any room. Available as kits, they come in two sizes.

The delight of the new and novel hooking-secret is a needle that cranks like an egg beater and makes up to 500 uniform loops per minute. Anyone can do it. It's so easy to use it's foolproof. Spacing of the loops is controlled automatically. The needle adjusts to three different heights of loops—medium height works best for rugs. An adjustable frame supports the rug as you work—frame keeps rug taut.

HOOKING RUGS

Rich colors, blue, bronze, mustard, and green abound on a white background in rug above. The colors are repeated lavishly throughout the hooked surface. A handsome subdued rug like this is relaxing in the sitting area of a bedroom or living room; it looks especially smart with furniture that is provincial or Early American.

Bold rug, upper right, provides a bright splash wherever you want to use it. Here, it beautifies an entry hall, gives an almost-Oriental look to the floor. A clear and crisp red emerges as a perfect contrast for its black, green counterparts. Design fits with contemporary, too.

A modern-day hooking bee in the family or game room is a pleasant way to spend a morning. It spells good fun, company, relaxation for group of family and friends.

This glowing rug, which goes so beautifully in front of a hearth, in a foyer, or on a porch, takes a lot of family living. The rich tones of yellow, bronze, gold, and white accent the dramatic olive that blends with almost any shade you can name; they add unusual depth to rug.

HOOKING IN A HURRY

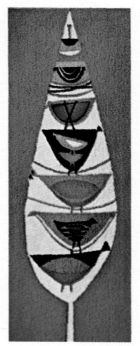

Rug hooking, always a beautiful craft but once painstakingly slow, is now ten times faster with a new needle that cranks like an egg beater. And the finished rugs lose none of their beauty in the speeding-up process. The needle works in any direction, making it easy to fill in intricate patterns quickly and accurately. It has an outer needle which opens a hole in the burlap; the inner needle forms uniform yarn loops. As you turn the handle, the needles work up and down and back and forth. It doesn't have to be pushed, just guided. You can reverse the direction of the needle whenever the pattern you are working on calls for it—going backward or forward by turning the handle the direction that is desired.

Hooking is a challenge to your imagination whether you use your own design or a kit like the ones pictured here. Hooked pieces that are shown here were made with an automatic hooking needle.

Though hooking is most often used for rugs, automatic needle lets you "paint" with yarn, as an artist does with oils. At far left below, rich blues, greens, and golds with black and white accents, make a trim contemporary wall hanging that could fit into many rooms.

For beauty at the bottom of a stairway, in an entrance hall, or beside a bed, try a double eagle pattern on a rug. The pattern is particularly good with Early American furnishings. Note, too, the cushion-size eagle that works equally well as pillow.

Low loops are best for pillow tops; medium-height loops for wall hangings, rugs. Highest loop is used for a handsome, dimensional look.

Perk up a room with a blaze of boldness. You'll be amazed at how quickly you can complete a hearthside rug of the size shown at left. There's no need to worry about depth of the pile when more than one person works on a rug during the course of its completion. The loop length is regulated by an adjustable set-screw in the automatic hooking needle.

To get a clear pattern on the right side of the piece you are working on, it is best to outline each design with one or two rows of stitches. You can then fill in the rest of the design by running rows of loops in the identical direction. When there are two colors next to each other, leave a little extra space. This gives clear color separation on the right side. This separation makes pattern distinct.

Another idea for hooking is to cover the top of a footstool for use in the living room. You can hook strong colors on a neutral background to give warm traditional look to a favorite footstool. Because it is less involved than the rugs, a design like this gives beginners a chance to experiment with the needle before attempting a rug or wall mural. Kit for a footstool cover would be a good starting point. In addition, you'd need needle, frame, table to work on, latex backing (for rugs and pillows). The designers of the rugs shown here: Jay and Bill Hinz, June Wischler Meyer.

PATTERNS FOR A BEDROOM

These versatile designs are adaptable to any size bed from twin to king- and queen-size. The dramatic motifs are easy to translate on the sewing machine, and a constant pleasure when completed. Once you've mastered the heirloom patterns you'll find they extend far beyond the bedstead. Use a part of the design for curtains, long or short. Touch dressing table skirts with nosegays. Or cover a rocking chair with a quaint cushion of tie-on shingles. There are endless possibilities for adjoining bathrooms like appliqued towels.

A regal combination of crowns, diamonds bedecks the subtle bedspread at left. Just vary textures and fabrics to complement your own choice in bedroom furnishings. It's a simple matter to adjust this pattern to today's wide choice in bed sizes. Add on extra rows for the "king," eliminate one line of the motif for a single-size spread.

For a time-saver, try cutting all of the crowns at one time, applique directly to the fabric, turning in the raw edges as you sew. Additional details on the spread are given on pages 146, 147. The designer was Jettie Penraat.

New coverlet is like spring clothes for a weary bedroom. This buttercup-bright coverlet, right top, is made with overlapping petals, machine-quilted and stitched to a medium-weight cotton bedspread. Petals follow one of the many coverlet patterns available. You'll find this equally effective in showy pinks, shades of burnished orange, or compelling magenta. For drama, back some of the petals with a contrasting shade.

It's versatile also. Try it in elegant taffetas for ornate decor—or, most charming of all, in a patchwork effect using scraps garnered from your dressmaking and sewing efforts. What if you later decide you want a different size bed? No problem. Just add extra petals.

Never a faded flower in the will-o'-the-wisp wall hanging turned headboard. Smooth-textured fabric works for background, then machine-appliqued bright blooms using a satin stitch at maximum width are added. A few deft touches can go on by hand. Designs are cut free-form—any arrangement that pleases you will give good effect. The greater the variety of fabric used, the more effective the applique becomes: blend coarse textures, waffle weaves, alluring velveteens into casual composition. Designer: Jean Laury.

QUILTING

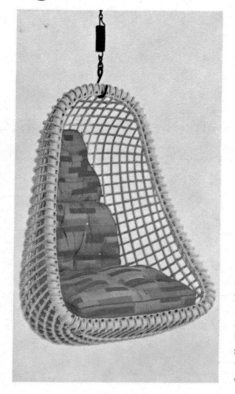

These lovely rainbow-hued samples of quilting are not complicated in color scheme or intricate in design. That's the delightful secret of this new and novel technique—there is no pattern. You're the designer, the designing was never easier. Your sewing machine slices away hours an all-made-by-hand coverlet would require.

These exquisite examples are marvels of simplicity. See complete how-to on page 148.

A rattan swinging chair picks up color of the coverlet, opposite. All of this fast quilting is done with the straight-forward stitch that is used to outline each block.

Sunburst shades are put to use in an eye-catching bedspread that is a coverlet by day, a quilt by night. Dominant red is picked up in the bolster, headboard, and dust ruffle. Don't stop here. Add other jewel-like color accents of quilted pieces.

Experiment with brilliant throw pillows on your sofa in the living room, a sweeping wall hanging, or a glorious parade of dining-room chair seats. Trim with color-keyed edging or ball fringe. This bedspread is trimmed with dramatic red ball fringe. Notice the additional uses of the trim on the bolster. Designer of spread shown here was Jean Ray Laury.

Vanity stool and wastebasket are slip-covered in fresh, wonderful colors. Intense aquamarines and relaxing cool blues are reflected in quilted panels on the handsome screen. Panels were studded in place with oversize brass upholstery tacks.

For all of these quilted beauties, just pick out co-ordinated fabric colors (we used 59-cent material from dress fabric counter), cut or tear the strips into appropriate lengths—and begin the modern quilting bee.

In the past, creative knitting was limited by the scarcity of yarn. Now, everyone from pre-teen to grandmother is knitting, stimulated by the abundance of exciting materials and the satisfactory results. Knitting for the home is soaring high in popularity at the present time.

The only supplies needed are a variety of knitting yarns, needles, and a knowledge of the basic stitches. Complete directions for reproducing any of the attractive designs assembled here are given on pages 150 to 153. The designer of these knitted items: Mary W. Phillips.

KNITTING

Cloud-soft afghan, right, goes with chair, sofa, or chaise. It is a blend of fluffy coral mohair and rust wool that knits up quickly. The finished afghan measures 48x65 inches.

The handsome wall hanging, knitted from synthetic straw, hangs over a piece of plain-color fabric. Alone, it works as a divider.

Bring a dining area up to date with handmade chair cushions and placemats. Tie-on cover, knitted here in turquoise, amethyst, blue, and black, can be knitted in any size, any colors. Slip-cover a pendant lighting fixture with linen yarn to hang at dining area.

A jewel-like array of brilliant throw pillows gives any room a lift. Covers, above, can be knit in a hurry and are an effective way to freshen older pillows. There's nothing special about yarn—it's standard knitting worsted.

Crocheting is a venerable art. It was used to add beauty and decoration to the homes of the first settlers of our country. Here, it's used in a fresh way. The basic crocheting stitches are the same, but there's a quick and easy way to applique them into a finished design. The trick is glue.

First, crochet yards of chains, braids, and fringes. Then apply trims to fabric—creating the designs as you work.

CROCHETING

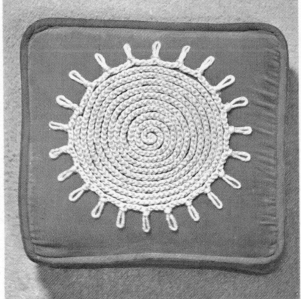

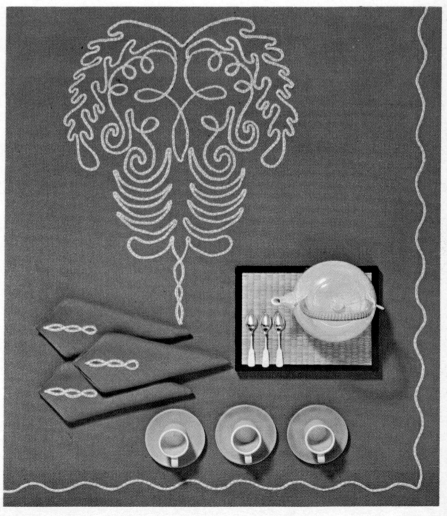

The handsome divider, far left, adds a note of textural beauty to a contemporary scheme, and breaks the openness of a large room. Silhouetted, crocheted motifs in graduated sizes were made from bulky homespun yarn, and then they were glued to a nubby linen for this effect.

Dress up a plain-color pillow by combining several crochet stitches. Or use one simple chain in your design. You may want to trim several pillows that blend in color and fabric. The type of adhesive you need will be determined by whether fabric must be laundered, dry cleaned.

A sophisticated scroll border on draperies or placemats can be created by crocheting a simple fringe from soft, bulky yarn. The scroll, above right, trims placemats. Make stitches over a wooden ruler. Then stitch or glue fringe on lines drawn around a teacup or bowl.

This fringe was left uncut, just as it comes off the ruler. For cut fringe, simply slit the loops with scissors. The amount of fringe you need will equal about double the length of the border that you wish to make.

A traditional table cover of washable linen is just right for a setting of any season. This design is placed on either end of the cloth. It could also be used effectively on a bedspread. It requires about 30 yards of single crochet chain. This design is made free-form—any pattern you like could be duplicated with this technique. The scroll border, which disguises seams, could also be used to give style to placemats. Designer: R. Wright. Additional details on crocheting are given on page 149.

YOUR OWN TOUCH ON SHEETS, PILLOWCASES, AND TOWELS

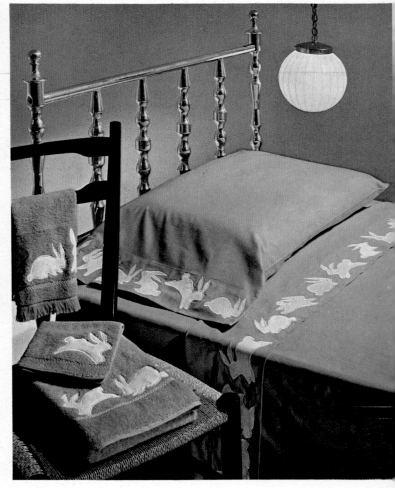

With a minimum of time and effort, you can apply clever designs on any plain-color sheets and towels. Only the simplest kind of machine stitching is needed for these designs that were done by Jean Ray Laury.

Birds on parade, above, are color coordinated, are perched facing both right and left. See how-to at right.

Scampering bunnies, right, make playful accent for child's room. The design gives custom appearance, is explained in detail on page 154.

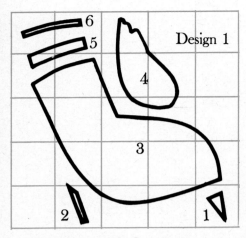

Design 1

APPLIQUE BIRD DESIGN

Materials needed; pillowcase, sheet, washcloth, and two towels. Choose contrasting colors for applique designs. Any soft fabric, such as cotton, appliques well. You'll need iron-on interfacing to place under applique fabric for machine sewing. Plan to use mercerized thread matching colors of appliques.

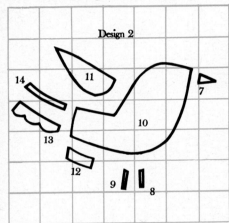

Design 2

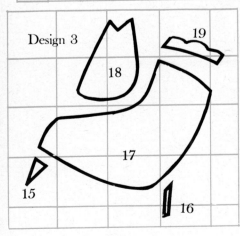

Design 3

DIRECTIONS: TO MACHINE STITCH PILLOWCASE

1. Expand designs to full size for patterns. For a pillowcase, you will need one of each of the five designs. When they are placed on the pillowcase, each design is centered along the hem area.
2. Bird designs face both right and left. Cut as pattern indicates. When cutting, be sure to place the applique patterns on right side of the fabric you use.
3. Apply iron-on interfacing to wrong side of fabric to be appliqued. The added stiffening will make machine appliqueing easier.
4. Cut out applique patterns, using one set for pillowcase (five bird designs), keeping each of the design units together.
5. Place patterns on applique fabric. Draw around patterns. Cut, following the drawn line, keeping each design unit together.

NOTE: Applique pieces are numbered and must be applied numerically to the fabric.

6. Pin each of one design unit on pillowcase following numerical order. Do all of first design before proceeding to other designs.
7. With thread matching each applique piece, machine stitch, using a satin stitch around each piece. Single line of stitching may be used for the birds' legs if you wish.

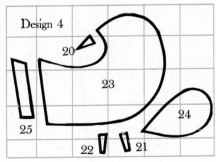

Design 4

1 square equals 1 inch.

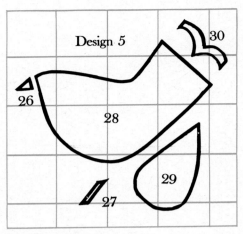

Design 5

BATH TOWEL

For a bath towel you will need for designs: Designs 1, 4, 3, 5. They will be put on bath towel edge in that order.

Repeat steps 2 and 3.

Cut out applique patterns for the four designs, keeping each design unit together for easy working.

Repeat steps 5, 6, 7 to finish towel.

HAND TOWEL

For a hand towel you will need three designs: Designs 2, 5, and 4. They will be put on hand towel edge in that order.

Repeat steps 2 and 3.

Cut out applique patterns for the three designs, keeping each design unit together for easy working.

Repeat steps 5, 6, 7 to finish.

WASHCLOTH

For a washcloth you will need one design: Design 1. This design is put just above any decorative border on cloth.

Repeat steps 2 and 3.

Cut out applique pattern for the design, keeping unit together. Repeat the steps 5, 6, 7 to finish the washcloth.

SHEET

When sheet is appliqued, designs will cover entire width of the sheet, centering patterns along the top hem area of the sheet. For sheet you will need on left half: Designs 1, 2, 3, 4, 5, 2, 3, 4. They will be put on left side in that order. For right side you will need: Designs 5, 4, 3, 2, 1, 5, 4, 3. They'll be put on right side in order.

Repeat steps 2 and 3.

Cut out patterns; cut required number of designs to cover entire width of sheet. Keep design units together.

Repeat steps 5, 6, 7 to finish sheet.

The fun and satisfaction of weaving comes in watching a beautifully colored and textured fabric grow from threads. You can make a beginner's loom for your weaving projects. The loom described here is an excellent one on which to begin weaving and is not difficult to make. On it you can make placemats, scarfs, towels, curtains.

WEAVING

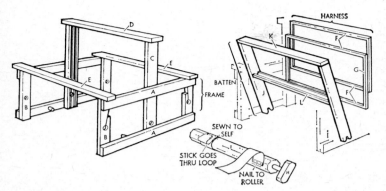

HARNESS

BATTEN FRAME

HARNESS

K

F

G

F

SEWN TO SELF

STICK GOES THRU LOOP

NAIL TO ROLLER

Buy 5' long 1"x12". Cut—
A- 4 pieces 1½"x19", top and bottom of loom frame
B- 4 pieces 1½"x8", frame ends
C- 2 pieces 2½"x15", harness guides
D- 1 piece 2½"x18½", harness guide top
E- 2 pieces 1½"x20", warp and cloth beams
H- 4 pieces 1½"x3¼", knobs—round edges
J- 2 pieces 1½"x11½", batten side pieces
K- 1 piece 1½"x17⅜", batten top
L- 1 piece 1½"x16", batten cross piece
Buy 2' long 2"x4". Cut—
I- 2 rollers. Rip 2"x4" in half, cut to 16¼". Cut off corners at 45° angle.
Buy 5' ½"x¾" window stripping. Cut—
F- 4 pieces 16½", harness top and bottom
G- 4 pieces 8¼", harness ends (may vary

slightly with length of heddles)
To order from loom supplier
15 dent reed 18" long
7" metal heddles
Supplies needed
M- ⅝" diameter dowel 18⅜" long
N- two ¾" dowels 2¼" long. O- two 4" long
P- two ⅜" diameter dowels 2" long
Two ¼"x2" carriage bolts; washers; wing nuts
12" of ⅛" aluminum clothesline wire
Two ⅛" screw eyes
28 #8 flat-head wood screws 1¼" long
Eight #6 round-head wood screws ½" long
Sixteen #17 brads ½" long
Four metal strips 1/16"x¼"x16"

A loom is a necessity for weaving. You can build a simple 2-harness loom following the directions given here. Listed above are the materials and supplies that are needed for the construction. Letters show location of each piece on the drawings. The directions also refer to pieces by letter.

If you would rather buy a loom, there are many fine sources and price ranges to choose from. Be sure the loom is made from hardwood and is sturdily constructed to withstand the pull of the tautly stretched threads and the continuous pounding of the beater.

Assembling the loom. Assemble right side of the loom frame using two A's and two B's. Drill ¾" holes through center of B's. Saw a cut 5" long on angle from top of piece through hole. Make a crosscut about 2½" from top to make notch. Assemble frame with notched edges of B in, using lap joints. Fasten with flat-head wood screws. Inside edges of A should be 5" apart.

Next, drill ⅝" hole through center of C, 1¾" up from bottom. Cut two ½" wide, ⅜" deep dadoes the length of C ½" in from each side. Center in frame with dado facing in. Fasten with screws. (See the top photograph at right.)

For left side of loom frame, drill holes only halfway through B's and C and omit saw cut and notch in B. Assemble as for right side.

Set frames upright and screw D to C to give correct spacing for warp and cloth beams. Screw E in place and then remove D.

Assemble harnesses with F and G, using #17 brads. There should be about ⅛" space at top and bottom of heddles when they are slid on metal strips and attached to the harness. (Actual measurement of the heddles may vary slightly and the length of G can be adjusted accordingly.) Cut notch in each end of metal strips, thread through eyes of heddles so all heddles face in the same direction. Fasten strips to harness with the round-head screws placed in notch. (See center photograph at right.) Slide harnesses in place in C.

The next step is making the harness lift mechanism. Drill ⅝" hole through center of a knob and ⅛" holes through each end in line with ⅝" hole. Slide M through hole in right C, through knob and into hole in left C. Slide knob to center of M. Drill ⅝" hole in center of another knob and glue to free end of M.

Cut aluminum wire in half and insert in lift knob of dowel. Place small screw eyes in center of lower edge of harnesses. Slip other ends of wire into the screw eyes and adjust so that the wires fit snugly—one harness will be up, the other down. Turn knob to force the wires into shape over the dowel. (See left bottom.)

For each roller, drill ¾" hole 1½" deep in each end of I. Glue N in one end of I. Pound nail in the other end of I 1¼" from end, through center of hole. This acts as a key in turning roller. Insert N in left B.

Cut 1" slot in end of O. Drill ¾" hole in knob and glue O into knob. Then slide slotted end of O through hole in right B and into I. (See the photograph above at right.) Note that the dowels holding rollers were not glued in place as the rollers must turn freely.

Drill ½" holes in right B midway along saw cut. Slide a carriage bolt into

hole with washer toward operator. Bolts permit adjustment of pressure on dowel holding the roller in the correct position for weaving.

Measure 5½" back from front edge and drill ⅜" hole in lower A on each side. Glue P in each hole to carry batten when it is finished.

Last unit of loom to make is batten. Cut ½" notches in bottom of J to fit over P. Cut dadoes ½" wide and ⅜" deep in center of K and L. Screw together J and K. Cut reed to fit inside frame and place top in dado in K. Attach L.

Cut 4 strips of heavy fabric, such as canvas, 2" wide and 8" long. Sew a 2" loop in one end of each piece. Nail other end to rollers, 2" in from ends of each roller. (See the drawing shown above.) From scrap lumber, cut two sticks ¼x½x15". Sand smooth and slip through fabric loops. Warp threads will be tied to these sticks. You will also

need to make from scrap, many shuttles and a beater stick. All should be ¼x¾x15". Shuttles have U-shaped notch in each end and beater stick has one end tapered to a point. All are sanded smooth. Keep your loom waxed with paste floor wax for easy operation.

WARPING THE LOOM

The first process in weaving is warping the loom. When you've completed this, the fabric is half finished.

Decide on the kind of material you want to work with, the color, and the number of yards of fabric you want to make. Firm cotton thread such as carpet weave is a good material with which to begin. To figure the amount of thread needed, first count the number of spaces in the reed you are using. A loom built from directions given on pages 26, 27 will have about 225 spaces. Multiply number of spaces by the length of material for yardage for warp thread.

When you get the amount of yardage needed for warp threads, double this figure and you will find the amount you need for the finished fabric. The first step: Get the number of the threads necessary to fill the reed, make each thread the same length. This is done with aid of a warping frame, right. Most common kind of a frame is a rectangular wooden one that's wide enough so that 1″ dowel rods set into two sides of the frame are 1 yard apart.

Warping frame, above, has two extra dowels in top row placed off-center to the left.

Suppose you plan to make 5 yards of fabric. Tie thread around dowel 5. Wind, as is shown in drawing, to dowel 1. Next wind thread up and over dowels 1 and 1A, and under 1B. Go around 1C, back over 1B, and under 1A. Then wind thread back down to dowel 5 where you began. When you've ten threads wound around dowel rod 1C, tie them together.

Each group of ten threads gives a count of twenty threads for a loom, since the yardage has been wound up one way, down other.

To use several colors in warp, break thread either where you begin winding (dowel 5) or at dowel 1C. To tie threads together, put ends together and knot. Be sure to keep knot close to end of peg. Remove any knots found in thread as you wind. Cut thread back to beginning or end of warp and tie on a new piece. Knots in middle of warp will show in the finished woven fabric. When you are done winding the number of threads you need, break thread and tie it to dowel 5 where you began winding. Tie piece of string about 6 inches down warp from 1A. Cut two straight sticks ½x½x12″ with holes drilled in each end, called lease sticks. Insert one in either side of cross formed by dowels 1A and 1B. Tie sticks together at each end through the holes that are drilled there.

To take warp off frame, begin at dowel 5. Slip threads off peg while grasping warp firmly about 12 inches from end. First tie near peg makes beginning loop through which another length of warp is drawn, like chain crochet. Draw up the loops until you reach lease sticks.

Tie lease sticks firmly at both ends to cloth beam of loom with short end of chain facing into loom. Remove heddles from frames by bowing bars out of the screws holding them to harnesses.

Starting at right end of groups of threads, pick out first thread. Every thread has a definite position and must be kept in place.

Push this loop through next to last slot in the reed. A reed hook or slim crochet hook will help. Pull the thread through reed and put over one end of

the stick that is inserted in cloth holders on other side of loom (see photograph at left below).

Take up next thread, and skipping one slot, insert in into second free slot. Continue in this manner across the reed using every other slot (only exception is a fine thread which is put through double in the reed; in this instance, use every slot).

When reed is threaded, slip on other cloth holder and begin winding the warp onto the warp roller. Wind clockwise so that the threads go under the roller and around (see photo above).

Wind only a little at a time—until you feel warp tense. Do not pull too tightly or you will break the threads. Tighten carriage bolts when you stop. Flat stick with tapered end (a beater stick) helps loosen knots which form along lease sticks. Loosen these knots and pull warp straight. Use stick to beat the warp as you would carpet.

If loom is placed up on table so chained warp falls loosely to floor, weight of material keeps tension even. Insert paper into warp beam roller as you roll up warp to keep different levels of thread from matting. Be sure sides do not slip off paper so they are shorter than middle of warp and cause the fabric to be crooked.

Stop rolling when the ends of threads are about 5 inches from lease sticks. Tighten down warp beam. Cut ends of threads off to same size as shortest end. Small difference in thread length is normal but if there's a difference of 6 inches or more, it would be wise to reroll your material.

Cut threads holding lease sticks to cloth beam but hold them tightly at the end so they do not slip. Set the stick closest to reed on edge. Half the threads are on the top edge and half fall below. Carefully edge stick up toward beater. Pull the warp tightly.

Looking through warp from side, you will see the "shed" which continues through reed and into back of loom. Put beater stick through shed. Make sure it corresponds exactly to stick in front and there are

no tangled threads in middle. Turn the beater stick on end (see drawing at left). Slip out lease stick (just the one) and put it in back next to the beater stick. Make sure they lay on same threads. Slip out beater stick and repeat with the remaining front lease stick.

Starting again from right side of loom, count off twenty threads and pull them out of the reed. Tie with loose slipknot. Continue across warp, tying each group of twenty. Put heddles in frames back on the loom. Because of crossed threads still held by lease sticks, you will be able to locate the first thread at right of warp. Put thread through eye of first heddle in front harness. Take up second thread. Put it through eye of first heddle in the back harness (see photograph below). Notice how one thread goes over one lease stick and under the other and second thread is just the reverse.

Check as you repeat process across the loom to be sure threads are in order. Retie the threads in twenties as you cross loom and let ends drop.

Last step is putting threads back into reed. Put one thread through every space since threads are now single. (If you are threading double with fine thread, put two in a space.) Start again at the right and repeat across.

Tie groups of twenty threads to stick which fits in cloth on roller in this manner: divide group of twenty into groups of ten. Holding the groups apart, tie as shown in the drawing at right. This is a weaver's knot and will hold your material securely. Make sure tension across the warp is even. Retie the groups if necessary to guarantee even tension.

When all threads are tied down, tighten cloth beam until the tension is firm and cinch down wing nut. Cut off lease sticks.

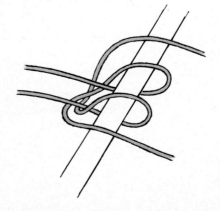

When the warping is finished, you're ready for the most enjoyable part of weaving—building a fabric. Here are directions for plain and fancy weaving and for finishing your fabric. The fabrics shown in the photograph above are: A—plain; B—plaid; C—leno; D—laid-in design.

Any of these weaves can be mastered on the loom that you built yourself, or on a simple loom that you purchased. Regardless of which weave you select, you'll find that the fabric will grow quickly for you.

BUILDING A FABRIC

Once the warping is finished, half the threads are in place. After the threads are tied on loom, tighten them down by leaving front wing nut secured while releasing the back nut and turning the back roller until threads are taut but not tense.

Pull the side lever toward you. Insert one of the lease sticks to beat the first thread against. Insert shuttle and push it through to the other side, leaving an end twice the width of your fabric.

Beat thread down with batten. Change to shed B by turning side lever away from you. Beat first thread once again. Insert shuttle; push through. That's all there is to basic or "tabby" weaving.

Shuttles should be almost as wide as the material you are making. You'll need three or four if you use several colors. They can be made from scrap lumber but they must be sanded until they are very smooth so they won't catch on threads as shuttles are pushed through the shed. To wind a shuttle, wrap thread around one end to hold it; then bring thread under top end and under bottom end in a figure 8 motion.

To add a new color, cut off old color at either end of a row, leaving an end about 2 inches long. When shed is changed for the next row, put this end that

Finish edges of fabric

is left through six or eight threads. It will be in same shed as the new color. Put second color through and leave a 2 inch end which is doubled back on next shed. Little tag ends can be cut off after the fabric has been washed.

After weaving two or three inches of material, finish off beginning edge of fabric. Same method is used for finishing at end of fabric or between pieces on loom.

Thread long end left at beginning of the fabric into a blunt tapestry needle. Go under first four threads on loom, up and over the same threads, then under again. Bring needle from underneath and through the fabric between second and the third rows.

This is step 1 of the finishing-off process. **For step 2,** put needle under the next four threads and up between second and third rows. Do not go around the threads, just go under them. Going across the row, go around threads twice (step 1) at the start. Work step 2 four times, then step 1 once, step 2 four times—continue this pattern. At the other end of the fabric, work step 2 twice and then fasten the thread.

Watch selvages of the fabric closely. If you pull on it too tightly, edges will be drawn in unevenly. It will take a bit of practice to make edges just right, but this is the mark of a good weaver. When the completed material gets close to the batten, move it down by releasing warp and cloth beams. Turn cloth beam, pulling newly woven material under cloth beam.

Tighten down the back nut. Pull the material so it is taut, and then tighten down the front catch. Now let's try some fancy stitches.

First let's consider a "leno" weave. It makes a lacy path across the plain or "tabby" weave.

Work back and forth three or five times across inch of warp. Then pick up three of the threads from bottom row of threads and bring them above top row of threads.

Now bring your finger between the bottom three threads and the next top three threads and let top threads drop below your finger. Continue across the row. Weave last inch plain. Change shed and

Leno weave

throw shuttle for one shot plain. Repeat twist, throw the shuttle, and continue with plain weave.

To make a monogram, or, practically

Wind with figure-8 motion

any pattern which can be drawn on graph paper, use the "laid-in" technique.

Using a contrasting thread, (it can be heavier as well), introduce it into the shed, bringing one end up and over the top threads where new color is to appear. In the same shed throw shuttle through, beat as usual.

On the next shed, pick up the contrasting thread and bring it up and over the top threads, widening or narrowing the color area just as you choose to do.

Throw the shuttle through again on the same shed. You can work out an endless variety of designs. It is best to work your design out on graph paper before you begin weaving it; that way you can avoid mistakes or avoid an unattractive pattern.

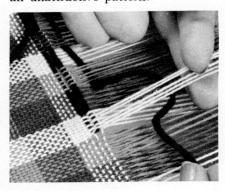

Laid-in design

These stitches are only two of the countless things you can do using your loom and your new-found weaving skill.

If you are interested in learning more about weaving and learning other stitches you can use, you will find excellent books that will provide you with more details, information at your library; or check with book dealer.

Plain or plaid weave goes quickly

To knit on loom, take up bottom thread with crochet hook. Pull loop over thread above it, drop on other side of nail. Repeat at each nail. Set up the threading pattern again. This time add only one row to get stacked thread effect. Knit off bottom threads as before. Continue till finished. Beginning on the right of loom, pick up the end stitch on one rail, drop over corresponding nail on opposite rail. Take lower thread, lift over upper thread; nail as in knitting. Repeat for each pair of nails. Begin again at right, take loop off first nail, drop over next. Knit off one thread. Take remaining loop off nail, drop over third nail. Continue to the last stitch, fasten as in regular needle knitting.

KNITTING SIMPLIFIED

The loom measures 3¾"x27½" and stands 4¼" tall. An uneven number (45) of No. 16 wire brads are spaced ½" apart across the loom with ½" distance between parallel nails.

The brads also extend ½" above the surface of the loom. To thread, use methods A or B that are illustrated at the right. Run the yarn over every other nail one way, then back over the empty ones. Repeat the process so there are two threads around each nail. Technique was developed for use by sixth grade in Monterey. Loom design was by Mildred Koch.

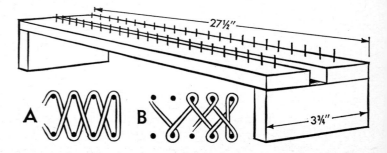

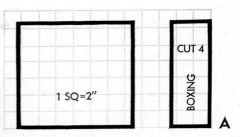

A

Striped pillow needs ⅔ yard of cotton, 4⅔ yards of bias tape. Cut following pattern A. Top-stitch tape in squares to cotton, mitering corners. First square is 1¾″ from raw edge. Others are 1″ apart. Seam boxing strip to trimmed square; seam boxing corners. Trim excess fabric. Seam plain fabric square to boxing on three sides; insert pillow. Tack.

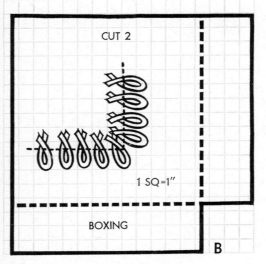

B

Square looped pillow uses ½ yard cotton, 25 yards each of two colors double-fold bias tape. Cut from B above. Start ¾″ from marked square, draw 8 squares ¾″ apart. Seam boxing strips. Cut tape into 3″ strips. Keep center fold on top, overlap ends, pin. Stitch on marked lines ¼″ from loop ends. Alternate colors on each side. Finish boxing, insert pillow.

Yellow loop pillow uses ½ yard cotton. Cut pattern C. Start 1″ from raw edges, mark triangle lines ¾″ apart. Cut double fold bias tape into 3″ lengths keeping colors separate. Form loops by overlapping ends at angle of markings. Stitch loops as in Pattern B. Tack center triangle of loops by hand in rows of five each, ½″ from stitching on previous row.

SEWING
FOR THE
HOME
CAN BE FUN

By using a little of your own creativeness when you are sewing accessories for the home, you'll find the task most enjoyable. Begin with tried and proven designs until you gain confidence in your own ability.

Then, take off on your own versions. Try the designs that are shown here; soon you'll be able to create your own. These decorative throw pillows can be used in your living room.

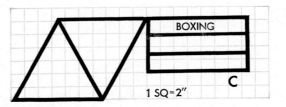

C

SUNNY STITCHING

A summer sunburst of brilliant canvas glorifies the garden and patio. All of these original designs that were created by Jean Ray Laury can be appliqued on ready-made covers or on new covers patterned from the old. Try gay flowers sprinkled on the covers and cloths, a series of radiating suns, apples, mushrooms, birds, or a profusion of pattern everywhere.

All will brighten your outdoor hours and will make your patio or garden look extra-special this summer. They are simple to sew. See complete directions given on pages 156 to 159.

A sun-drenched deck may burn bare toes, so spread out the sunning mats.

Stretch on these for tanning, to dry off after a swim, or to soak up sun. Cut full-width long ones for adults . . . shorter ones for the smaller tots. These, along with the covered-in-canvas polyfoam pillows, invite relaxation.

A patio supper party, right, features an expandable tablecloth that's as "at home" indoors as out. A smaller version of design may be done on napkins.

Machine-appliqued flowers, made of acrylic canvas, are echoed in beach umbrella. A pointed center sup-

port permits the umbrella to be set into the ground anywhere—offering transportable shade around the yard or at the beach or poolside. The rib ends of the umbrella are adorned with bright red rubber balls that add gay look.

The swinging circle chair, a real favorite with younger members of the family as well as adventuresome adults, boasts a brilliant sunflower with stem and leaves.

Stem grows up from the center seam, while the seat is covered with appliqued roots. Traditional yellow, green, and white color scheme for flower goes well with canvas.

A summery sun-and-shadow look extends a delightful invitation to quiet contemplation at garden pool.

Watching from the back of one circle chair, a colorful bird overlooks her nest of eggs, appliqued onto the seat. A red and orange sunflower is trim on other circle. And you have Victorian elegance for the always popular butterfly chair. Applique designs, also cut from canvas, are machine sewed with a full-width satin stitch. Bold colored banners serve as sun seats—for perching at the edge of pool.

Directors' chairs, right, take on a new and glamorous air to perk up a patio. The enamel finishes and synthetic canvas are keyed to light and bright colors. As folding chairs, they work indoors too. Acrylic canvas is fadeproof and easily washable—it does not shrink or stretch. Ready-mades slip on or off easily, making it simple to add new patterns.

CREWEL AND TENERIFFE

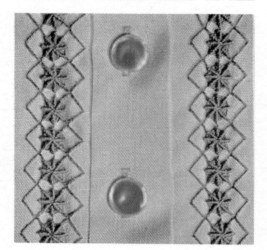

Anyone who can handle a needle can master the simple basic crewel or teneriffe embroidery illustrated here. Crewel embroidery, which originated in England over 300 years ago, combines many stitches, each easy to master. Crewel usually is worked on linen.

Teneriffe embroidery gets its name from teneriffe lace which it closely resembles in looks and technique. Both the lace and embroidery are worked in the same way—from the center out, like a spider's web. To give a three-dimensional look, pearl cotton is used instead of the ordinary embroidery floss.

Crewel and teneriffe can be used effectively to trim plain ready-mades. You'll get a one-of-a-kind look for your fashions. Or, use these techniques on guest towels, on pillow covers.

Notable two-piecer, below left, has a detailed overblouse that is bordered with delicate teneriffe. Try this border on placemats, napkins, runners, or cafe curtains, too, for a truly distinctive look. The complete details on this design and others shown here are given on pages 160 through 163.

Round out a little girl's wardrobe with a dark cotton for parties or playtime. This easy teneriffe embroidery flatters an inexpensive dress. Place pinwheels at random; vary the colors for a finished rainbow effect.

Teneriffe works up quickly on any fabric.

Look what you can do to give unadorned ready-made fashions a feminine flourish.

The crewel or teneriffe work will be more outstanding on a clean-line, simple dress.

Dress up a plain-color frock with colorful crewel flowers, left. This design makes use of many stitches, will be a display of your talent. Experiment with the design as a scroll border on your sheets or towels, or, do a scaled-down version on a handkerchief you intend as a special gift.

Animals figure prominently in crewel embroidery. This squirrel, below, is real favorite with children. The shaded effect is created by using three colors of embroidery floss. Design could be worked on a hat or a matching headband for little girl.

Cleverly-styled sheath is enriched with appropriate detail around the pockets. The design can be repeated again and again on dinner-size tablecloth and on napkins.

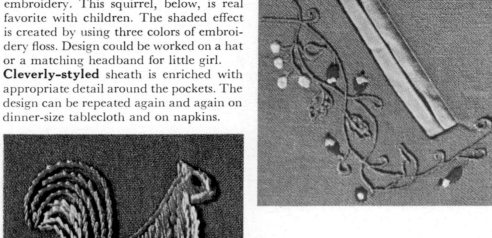

EMBROIDERY

Drawings of flowers and fruits make perfect designs for embroidery. They abound in books, old herbals, prints, magazines—and most of them need little pruning or rearranging for embroidery.

Trim off the extras, such as unwanted leaves or roots when you trace the drawings for your use.

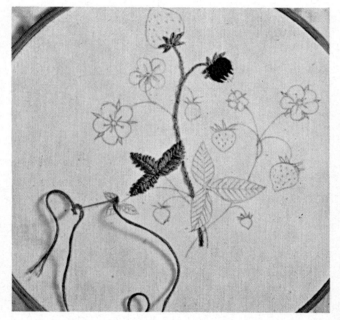

This embroidery is done by using six-strand embroidery floss. If you prefer, the strands can be divided for finer work. Stitches and other designs are explained in detail on pages 162 to 165.

When embroidering, work each stitch in separate movements: one up, the other down, rather than both at the same time. To avoid knots in finished work, make a knot in the end of thread; pass needle down through fabric about an inch away from where you mean to start embroidering. Next, take it up to the starting point of the stitches in question. Knot and then cut the excess thread after your stitches are started.

Strawberry cluster is ready for you to trace full size on fabric of your choice. It was designed for a placemat but would be nice embroidered on apron, towel set, too.

Notice how well the stitches express the textures—a smooth satin-stitch for the petals, long-and-short ones for bumpy berries. Slanted satin-stitch gives a notched effect to the leaves, split-stitch sturdiness to stems.

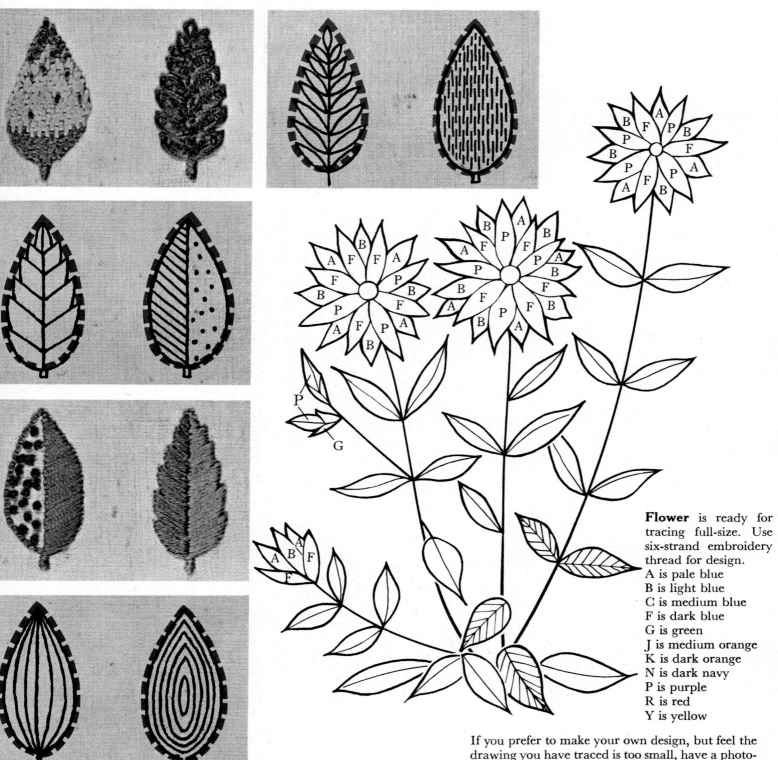

Flower is ready for tracing full-size. Use six-strand embroidery thread for design.
A is pale blue
B is light blue
C is medium blue
F is dark blue
G is green
J is medium orange
K is dark orange
N is dark navy
P is purple
R is red
Y is yellow

The leaf designs shown here illustrate how this same shape (see dotted lines), can be varied by stitches used. This may become a design in itself for use along the edge of a placemat or on a pillow top. If you wish, you could make 'a border of leaves to use along the edge of a towel— simply trace on huck toweling.

If you prefer to make your own design, but feel the drawing you have traced is too small, have a photostatic copy made and enlarged to the size you wish. This is not an expensive service; for little money you can have it enlarged from original negative to several different sizes for various purposes.

After your design has been perfected to size you wish, make a tracing of it on thin paper with 2H pencil. For transferring to fabric, turn penciled drawing face down on cloth; drip a puddle of lighter fluid on back. While it is still wet, rub over with edge of spoon. (Use small amount at time. Do not inhale fumes. Don't use in cold, dry room).

Several impressions can usually be made from a single drawing before it must be repenciled. If you wish to reverse the design, simply trace the pencil lines on the other side of tracing and proceed.

Flower and leaf motifs decorate the contemporary wall hanging, left, that has marine-green felt background that measures 20"x 56". Space of backing is broken with elongated rectangle of tan felt. Dull yellow-green rectangle of felt is superimposed on the tan, then repeated at right top.

Long rectangular shape is repeated in dull red felt. And the dark purple felt rectangle with corner cut away is positioned at bottom of wall hanging.

Pieces were all placed in position, pinned securely, basted to hold. Then edges are attached to background with a buttonhole stitch using two strands of six-stranded embroidery floss.

The long line in the center is made of wool yarn in single crochet stitch, then a treble stitch, and finally another treble stitch. All strips are fastened to background with a running stitch of floss. After crocheting is positioned, all 1" loops are pinned in place, then they are attached with couching stitches.

Loops for all flowers are shaped with the fingers, pinned in place, and then secured with couching stitches using two strands of floss. Stems for the three rosettes on the felt are made of two strings of wool thread secured first by pins, then with couching stitches. Centers are made of small bundles of wool yarn that are tied in the center with a long piece of thinner wool yarn, then needled through and tied on the back. Some are clipped to form balls, others are left with the loops showing.

Solid centers of the flowers are made by coiling the thread in the fingers in a flat spiral, then pinning the spiral down, couching all pieces securely with two strands of floss. Loops around the spirals are first pinned, then are neatly couched to secure them firmly to the background.

The stem of the plant on the green felt is made of single crochet stitches and treble stitches. Stems at the side are only single crochet stitches. The leaves are pinned in place, then are secured with couching stitches.

The zigzag line was pinned, attached in place using couching stitches. Small tan circles of felt are appliqued using buttonhole stitches. The tiny red circles are felt attached with series of cross stitches in the center.

EMBROIDERED WALL HANGINGS

Felt birds fly over a colorful flower tree in the wall hanging on the opposite page. Even the green grass below exhibits a sprightly design, adds to the total effect of traditional charm.

Background of homespun fabric measures 20″ by 56″. It has a 3″ slot for a wood slat at the top and a 5½″ wide hem at the bottom. In spite of its size, the wall hanging is light enough to go easily on any wall in the home.

The birds of red and/or orange and black felt measure about 3″ by 2½″ each. Cut them free-form, letting half of the birds face one way, half face the other way. Wings should be tilted at a "flying angle." Be sure to add eyes, top-knot at the heads, and beaks.

The birds and green felt stems at the bottom of hanging hand-tack in place using fine stitches.

Tree stands about 28″ tall. Trunk and branches of purple felt secure by blanket stitches to backing. Flowers range from 1½″ to 4″ in diameter. Larger ones and some small ones attach to backing by blanket stitches; smaller ones attach in center only. Others secure by couched coils of yarn. Clipped and unclipped tassels center each flower. The tiny felt flowers at the base of tree are hand-tacked in position.

Gold hanging, left, doubles as a handy stole. It has a satin lining and outside measurements of 12″x 36″. Fabric was woven, but any heavy-body material would work equally well. Multicolored yarn flowers combine lazy daisy and cross stitches; a French knot centers each of the flowers.

The wavy lines are easily achieved by fine running stitches of royal blue crochet thread laced with purple or blue colored yarn. The spaces between flowers are dotted with French knots. The stole or wall hanging is then lined with a soft, gold satin using a simple hemming stitch.

Maroon and purple wall hanging, at right, has corduroy framing background of men's suit interlining and attaching to denim lining on three sides.

Corduroy pieces in design are appliqued with blanket stitches. Border is finished with feather stitches. Each of the flowers and leaves is made on separate piece of interlining, cut around, finished with blanket stitches, then hand-tacked to secure.

Leaf shapes have chain stitch veins, some are accented by French knots, others by lazy daisy stitches. Rippled flowers combine cretan stitches with French knots, or chain stitches with French knots and with lazy daisy stitches. Crochet thread and yarn interchange often, resulting in delightful texture, color, and depth for the wall hanging. You may use any closely-related color scheme to get this same effect.

Green felt bordered potted flower, below, measures 8¾″ wide and 11¾″ long. Felt flower has diameter of 4″ and leaves extend 3½″.

Felt flower attaches to linen background with crochet thread in feather stitch.

Lazy daisy stitch in crochet thread makes design on the leaves. Couching and chain stitches trim pot.

Colorful flower composition, left, would be ideal in bedroom, a hallway, or any place you need an individual look, color accent.

Children, too, would appreciate a personalized picture for their own to treasure now and in years to come.

This flower picture measures 13″x16″ from frame edge to edge.

EMBROIDERED WALL HANGINGS

A royal blue yard border runs all the way around the burlap background. The border is a running stitch, accented with a scallop lacing.

The tiny birds of felt have triangular orange bodies and round red heads. Blue crochet thread appliques birds using the blanket stitch.

French knots form eyes. Green felt makes stems and leaves for the flowers appliqued to background by various colors of crochet thread. The flowers are decorated by the lazy daisy stitch using a variety of colors of thread.

Orange felt flowers and the buds are trimmed with royal blue felt circles and then are edged in royal blue yarn French knots. Lazy daisy stitches create a pattern on each in crochet thread.

Abstract sampler, left, made by Zanne Meyers, shows design that developed in natural way. The top of the panel contains many repeats of the simplest of embroidery stitches. More complex ones, like couching, were added to bottom of sampler.

To adapt this idea, you'll need a piece of coarse linen, assorted yarns, threads, and even string and clothesline. Allow ½ inch for framing.

Elongated flower picture, left, measures 9¼″x21″. Felt flowers range from 3¾″ to 1½″ in diameter, beginning at the bottom. Colors of flowers beginning at the bottom include purple, royal blue, and red; also red-orange, yellow, and orange. Flowers attach to the loosely woven beige background using a cretan stitch in black yarn (for bottom four) or the feather stitch (for the top four). The tiny green felt circles are held on by cross stitches. The lazy daisy stitch attaches green leaves.

Orange, red, and yellow French knots center flowers which are encircled by couching. Stems and base are created by the chain stitch. Orange crochet thread laces beneath black yarn on the twin flowers at the bottom of the design. Designs are by Roena Clement.

CRAFTS

Handcrafted items beautify homes in a unique way. Some are of the quality that will qualify them as collectors' prizes at a future date; others offer more temporary pleasure, being created for the fun of it.

Craft materials show the greatest variety ever—hobby shops and art supply dealers carry the newest craft plastics, brilliant papers and paints, and all the efficient protective sprays and handy tools. What you use and what you create is up to you. There's no right or wrong connected with craft techniques.

Designs made with embroidery thread or yarn are smart and inexpensive. Either of these well-known craft materials can be used for items suitable to any kind of decorating scheme.

Use a needle and embroidery stitches if you wish. Or, you can do modern "stitching" with white glue.

The four designs at right consist of embroidery thread glued to illustration board. To duplicate this effect, buy a set of unfinished frames.

Cut pieces of illustration board to fit frames. Using a pencil, lightly sketch drawings on boards. Then use a clear-drying glue to outline small section. Glue on strand of thread. Work until all of design, background is full. Paint the frames to match.

Yarn wall hanging, left, has burlap background. Fabric is stapled on back side to a piece of heavy illustration board. When the burlap is taut, start arranging the yarn strands on front.

When the yarn falls into a design that pleases you it is ready to glue down.

Glue a small portion of the design at a time to keep the pattern intact. Use two or more closely related colors. Designer: C. Harvey.

FABRIC COLLAGES

To create a fabric collage, you will need scissors and fabric, fabric glue from an art shop, dry-mounting paper from an art or photo shop, and pressed board.

First, determine the size you want hanging to be, have pressed board cut to size. Cut background fabric to measurement, apply an inch of fabric glue to board at top. Anchor background. Roll remaining fabric forward to attach. Glue about 4 inches at a time. When background is firm you are ready to attach the details of the design.

Small pieces of leftover fabric make collage at far left. The designer Don Werner created design using a panel of striped fabric to cover one-third of the width—a good proportion for design.

This collage was made from remnants from eating area drapery fabric—plus material left over from sewing projects. Another good source is the remnant section of department store—you can count on finding bargains.

Use of pattern on pattern gives a rich effect to gold collage, center.

Several small-pattern fabrics combine successfully here. Background material sets the pace with subtle, tone-on-tone look. Deeper golds and browns stand out against it. To complete design, vivid blue-and-red fabric was used at vital points. An intricate design like this takes a little longer to mount, but finished look makes it worthwhile.

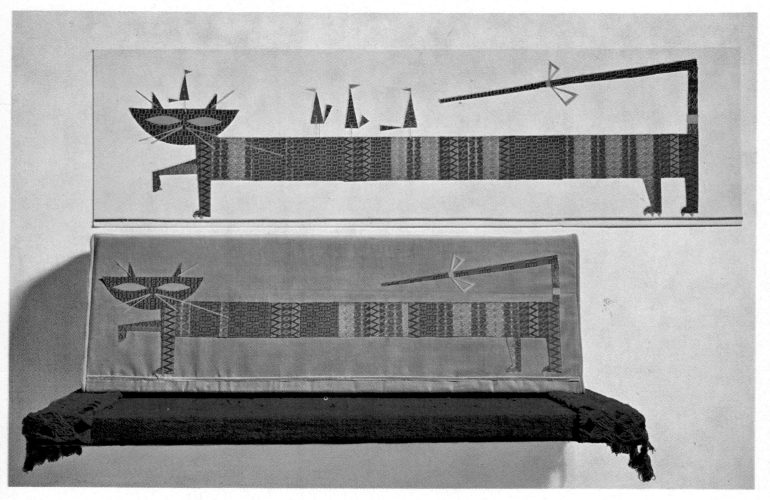

Brilliant colors of patterned fabric make these stylized cats double daring. The heads are half circles of fabric, bodies and legs are shaped from rectangles, the ears and toenails are triangles. The bird friends perched on back of one cat also have shape of triangles.

The individual trimming details are added last. Cording and braids, such as are available in notions departments of stores, are ideal for use as long lines.

The individual parts of the fabric designs were attached to the background fabric with dry-mount paper. To attach the first design piece, place the wrong side of your design fabric on the dry-mount paper; rub lightly with palm of your hand until fabric sticks.

Then, cut out the shape. Repeat for each of the design pieces you will need.

The design pieces now have a paper backing. As you cut, you'll find that the scissors action will bond the edges.

Place the cut designs on the background fabric, working in order that they go on the design.

To attach a design piece, place the bonded piece in the exact position it will fill on the collage. Cover it with tissue paper to avoid direct contact with heat. Then press carefully with a hand iron. Working slowly and easily, move the warm (not hot) iron over the surface of the design, using a little bit of extra pressure on the edges of the fabric piece. Work to avoid wrinkles.

Working with paper is one of the most imaginative crafts you could try. Paper designs can contain a big enough surplus of color and texture to interest and intrigue your family and friends for weeks. It's an inexpensive craft—the tools you need include a pencil, scissors, a ruler, various adhesives, clear spray lacquer, artist's knife, and of course, paper.

Art-supply dealers have a wonderful supply of tissue and other papers—and, your dealer will advise you on best glues and sprays to use.

PAPER DESIGNS

Stained glass panels, above, can bring brilliant beauty to a kitchen or an adjoining living area. The designs are formed by triangles and other basic shapes of colored tissues, overlaid on each other. First, cover glass with desired base color of tissue; apply with a clear spray. Do not trim edges until you have completed your design. Lay on shapes, one at a time. Secure with spray and then smooth with fingers. When design is dry, trim the edges.

The pretty paper plaid covers large coffee can. Tissue strips are applied vertically, then horizontally. Finish edges of the can, top and bottom, with gay ribbon.

Paper posy, left, is made of luscious colored tissue paper. You may wish to do a series of fancy flowers, even switching kinds of paper. Try construction paper or a corrugated cardboard. Add whimsical feather.

The design on the tray shown was planned so the separate areas of color set off spaces for a plate, cup and saucer, and glass of a place setting. You start with a piece of foil the same size as tray. Decorate with tissue. To finish, spray with water-resistant clear spray.

One way to make a paper flower is to cut circles to the size desired for finished blossom. Fold into equal parts; form a circular-topped triangle. Cut triangular shapes (A) in top for petals; rounded shape (B) for center. Glue center to illustration-board background. Add many layers of circles. Cup petal fringe forward. Spray. Add a yarn stem. Or add piece that was accordion pleated, cut.

These cutting techniques couldn't be simpler; yet they add a professional look to the finished product. As a starting point, why not try cutting experiments with common basic shapes. Circles are one of the three basic forms you can cut apart to create an abstract shape. Using a scissors, split circle into straight-line sections without adding to or subtracting from the basic form. After you have done this, move the pieces to expand them into a new, cut-apart shape.

When the proportion of extended circle pleases you, it is ready to paste onto white paper. Repeat for extra practice and for addition of new layers to your design.

You'll be amazed at how much difference just a little variance in the basic shape will make for the finished design. Try an oval for the next project. The oval expands into a longer, and, in some ways, more graceful design after it has been cut. This is particularly good on long, oblong wall hangings, or even on oval designs.

Rectangles, from symmetrical squares to the greatly elongated sizes, offer endless possibilities for abstract experiments. Gradually, as you cut and work with arrangements from several rectangles, try moving the forms just a little out of the original context. The resulting design will still look related, yet be more interesting.

For the best results, train your hands to make rhythmical, long cuts when you're cutting apart any of these basic shapes. Short, choppy pieces are seldom as pleasing to the eye. Do not allow any jagged edges on pieces.

Triangles are interesting forms that are the behind-the-scene secret of many of the most unusual designs cut from paper. The triangle shape itself is unique.

When you practice with triangles, manipulate the scissors to produce graceful, curved cuts. When you move the pieces out of context to a slight degree, you will find that your eyes still can recognize the basic outline.

Style-leading decorations lend a look of personalized beauty that's easily recognized. It's not at all important whether this look comes in the form of a traditional wall hanging cut from calico-printed wallpaper or from a paper posy cut with a space-age flair. To boast real style, decorations need the unexpected. They need a real freshness that's theirs alone. Don't be afraid to team more than one basic shape into a single decoration. Do check the design as you go along to be sure the effect is still pleasing. Practice will help develop more skill.

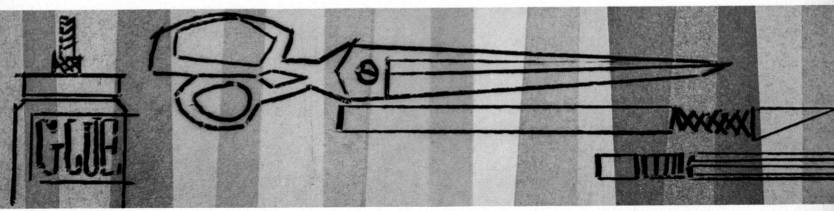

Inexpensive papers come in rainbow colors, are ready for you to use to decorate trays, make pictures, or trim food cans. You can duplicate the design effects shown here, or strike out on your own and create whatever effect you wish. Each person sees thing through individual eyes, so the finished result should represent you—should be indicative of your taste and color preferences.

If you tire of a design made of paper, you can always add new layers in the future and vary the effect until you find just exactly the one that pleases you. Or, with an inexpensive wall hanging like the paper posy, you can well afford to completely start over—just for fun of it.

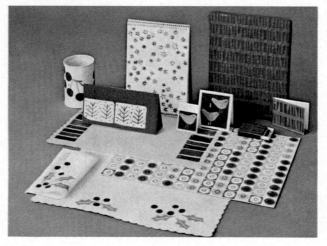

BUSY WORK
FOR
LITTLE HANDS
AND
BIG ONES, TOO

The simplest crafts are fine fun for the youngest members of the family—and, you'll find you enjoy helping them, too. Try making stamped trims or glamorous white birds on the next rainy day when play outdoors is impossible. Or, let young ones help trim Christmas papers.

Art gum printing, shown at left, is just as satisfying as finger painting and far less messy. Two young experts try their hand at this intriguing new craft. To make designs on gum erasers, first draw outline, then cut away the unneeded areas, leaving only the raised printing surface. Cover the surface with paint and stamp it on note paper, gift wrap, or on desk accessories like those shown.

Let the designs take the form of all-season medallions, fancy short stripes, stars, birds, stylized trees, holly, fruit, or any item with a simple outline that strikes your fancy.

Flocks of birds can be created as a family project. They are all cut from light construction paper. The bodies are in one of the pieces, the wings in another. The outline is so simple that even a four-year-old will have no trouble following lines.

Using the pattern given here, cut wings and bird's body from one sheet of paper.

Fold wing in center and glue to body. Attach wire for hanging.

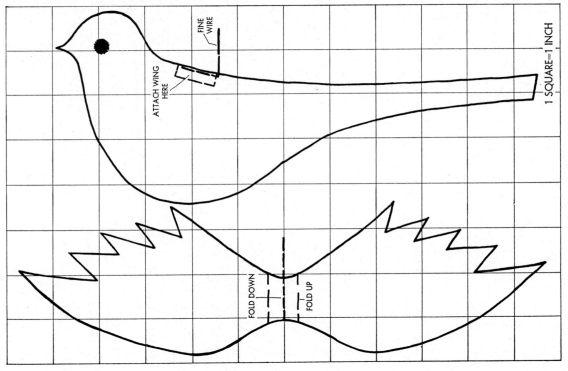

FINE WIRE

ATTACH WING HERE

1 SQUARE=1 INCH

FOLD DOWN

FOLD UP

Bright felt flowers can be used on variety of backgrounds to display them effectively.

Try them on boards covered with felt, burlap. Or, put a colorful collection of them on a painted rattan mat and use as a holiday wreath. The flowers, designed by Gladys Herndon, make good package trims, too.

FELT TRIMS

Wall tree, left, consists of a 22- by 31-inch panel of composition board, or a heavy corrugated cardboard may be used. Soft wood also is acceptable, but the cardboard or composition board will be more manageable for cutting and for pinning flowers.

Cover panels with burlap, pulling fabric to the back and taping or stapling it to hold. Attach the burlap-covered panel to a slightly larger cardboard covered with felt.

For the flowers, cut multicolored swatches of felt into circles ranging in sizes from 1 inch to 3 inches. Snip into circles to form points or petals to get a variety of flower shapes. Center some of the flowers with plain circles of smaller size, different color. Pin flowers to the background at different heights using hatpins. The flowers may be juggled until a satisfactory design is achieved.

A flower-decked wreath, right, consists of a 12-inch diameter plastic-foam doughnut cut flat on back side. Base is concealed with strips of complementary green crepe paper glued to hold. After wreath is covered, wire it to greenpainted rattan mat.

The plastic-foam base is ideal for holding the pinned flowers. These blooms are of bright shades of red, yellow, orange, and pink. Flowers are made following the same technique described for the wall panel. Flowers vary in diameter from 1 to 3 inches.

Flower tree is a fine family project. Dad can build the background; Mother and boys and girls can cover the panels, cut and create the felt flowers to pin in place once the panels are finished. The flowers push into supporting background at various depths; edges overlap.

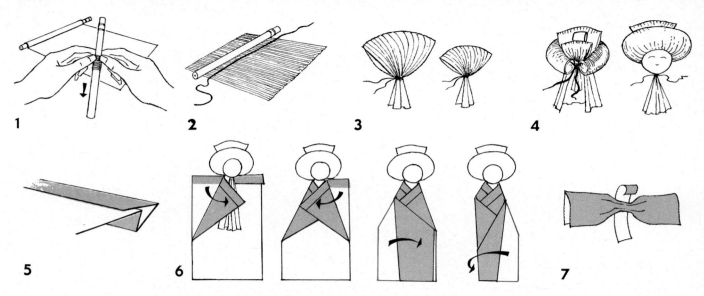

ORIGAMI

This fascinating paper-folding craft comes from Japan where children learn it in school. You'll enjoy making these, too. **Step-by-step** directions for making a geisha doll are shown above. For a 12-inch doll, cut a piece of white tissue paper so it is 9 inches wide and 12 inches long.

Roll it around a pencil; push the paper down from the top till it wrinkles tightly. This is illustrated in step 1. Repeat with 2x9 inch and 1½x9 inch pieces. Lay string across large piece of paper and roll it to within 4 inches of the end, stuffing with cotton (2). Put cotton in small pieces of tissue, fold over and tie (3). Place small rolls inside larger with bit of print paper between small rolls; tie. In front, stuff cotton in ruffle of paper under roll, tie to form face, neck (4). Cut flowered paper 8x10 inches. At top, fold 1 inch back, then bring ½ inch back over to front (5). Lay head on paper, fold as shown (6). Repeat with sheet of colored or printed paper. For obi, paste 1x5 inch piece of printed paper around figure. Fold 2x5 inch piece in half, wrap ½ inch wide strip around it, then paste in back so ends show from front. The hair is painted with black tempera paint.

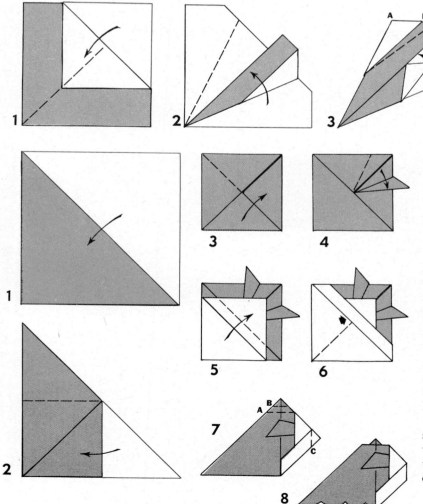

Easy-to-fold parrot is made following the directions (1 through 5) shown above. First, crease paper diagonally to mark the center. Fold corner over with the colored sides together (1). Fold edges in to the center (2); fold edges AB in to center (3). Bring the top ends down, out on the dotted line (4). Fold figure in half at original crease. Fold point back to shape head.

Try a goldfish next. Fold paper in half with colored sides out (1). Bring folded edges down to center (2). Fold top flaps up (3); then fold edges of flaps back from center (4). Bring top sheet of lower section up, crease (5). Fold same piece up again. Slip finger in pocket at arrow, lift and flatten figure on dotted line (6). Fold triangle at A down, then fold point up at B. Fold over at C (7); cut fin shapes (8).

The bird and fish can be made from any size square. Origami paper is best to work with, but lightweight typing paper may be used. Origami paper is available at larger department stores as are books on origami.

CRAYON CRAFTS

Landmarks of cities of the world make fascinating "ingredients" for picture collages that use crayon techniques. These three, illustrating three of the major cities of the world, show how colorful the results can be. To reproduce one of these or to create your own design, choose an interesting city, make sketches of identifying buildings, scenes, or people, then combine the sketches in a collage.

Three different techniques were used for these three examples. The city of Istanbul uses a crayon overlay technique; the city of Tokyo uses a crayon scratchboard; city of Rome, crayon transfergraph.

The city of Tokyo, far left, shows scratchboard to advantage. In scratchboard all areas in design are outlined in pencil. When the design is considered pleasing, the pencil lines are re-drawn using India ink with a rather wide nib pen. The width of line is determined by the size and intricacy of the design.

When the ink lines are dry, wax crayon is used heavily in each space. Then, a thin coat of tempera paint or India ink is applied over the design. It can be brushed on easily by using soap on the brush occasionally while you are painting. Or, it can be rubbed on with soft cloth.

Overcoat is then scratched off with pointed tools such as pens, styluses, combs.

The city of Rome, left, is done crayon transfergraph. In transfergraph, colors needed for anticipated composition are decided upon first. Then color sheet is made ready for transfer to another paper.

Transfer accounts for delightful and unique color and texture effects in design.

To begin a transfergraph, apply colored chalk rather heavily to a sheet of drawing paper. Paper used can be any paper having enough texture to hold a firm application of chalk. Next, apply a layer of white wax crayon over the chalk. Then add another layer of wax crayon over white

layer. Decide upon the color of this layer in preliminary planning. If a dark value of the chalk is desired, the final color can be black. However, you may achieve some surprising results when different wax crayon colors, as well as similar ones, are used in combination with most any color of chalk.

When preparatory sheet is ready, place a sheet of paper on it. Use poster, unprinted newspaper, typing, or ledger paper. A sketch of the design can be drawn on the back of smooth transfer sheet.

Use fairly hard pencil or stylus to draw or redraw design on back of sheet. This transfers color to smooth paper. Or, place color sheet face down on smooth surface, draw design on back of color sheet. Use this approach if lettering is part of design.

City of Istanbul, right, was first painted with smooth, flat tempera. Small details need not be included in underpainting. When paint dries, wax crayon is applied heavily over all areas.

After applying crayon overlay, begin scraping it off in varying degrees. Use "tools" around the home such as table knives, tongue depressors, or nail files. The tool, the way it is used, and the extent the wax crayon is removed determines color, texture, and amount of detail and design.

SUMMER

WALL PLAQUES

To duplicate the wall plaques, use the charts on the opposite page to discover what method is used to make each flower, plus trims used, and general tips on shaping each flower.

Remember to count points on only one side of rickrack whenever a number is indicated. Yardage is for one flower or leaf, unless indicated otherwise. Use matching heavy thread for gathering. Glue the flowers in place if you wish. Frame, then hang.

WINTER

SPRING

TACKING

Seam ends of rickrack together to form ring. Use five rickrack points. Tack 5 inner points together.

INTERLOCKING

Fold rickrack in half, or join two colors of same length, interlock by hooking V's together. Press flat.

A. Start with raw ends of folded and interlocked rickrack and roll on itself between fingers. Tack folded end and underside to retain shape. For full bloom rose, fold back outer rim of points. For cabbage rose, tack bud, then continue rolling loosely, tacking outer edge to fabric.

B. Interlock rickrack. Using a running stitch through points on one edge, draw thread to gather.

LEAVES

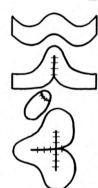

A. Single leaf or calyx: Cut the W from the rickrack. Stitch together lower V. Fold the ends in. Turn to right side, then secure.

B. Leaf cluster: Cut three or five points of rickrack. Seam ends to form ring. Stitch together lower V's. Turn right side and secure tightly.

STEMS

A. Corded piping: Draw design on fabric. Stitch piping to design. Cut away excess piping seam allowance. Turn cording over to cover stitches, tack to fabric. Remove excess seam allowance from piping, glue to the design. Cut the hidden edges.

B. Baby rickrack: Stitch through rickrack center to design, or glue.

C. Tubing: Draw design on fabric. Baste through tubing. Tack on wrong side over basting. Remove basting. Can be glued to design. Remove ½″ filler cord from exposed end.

Right Side

Wrong Side

GATHERING

For ease in stitching and forming each flower, let rickrack points build up on needle in a group, then draw snugly. Repeat as needed. End securely and tack the ends.

A. Stitch through rickrack center.

B. Fold rickrack in half with the points matching. Stitch into one point and out the next point.

C. Use one row rickrack; repeat B.

D. Stitch in and out of each point. Keep petal points in one direction, tack outer points to fabric.

E. Use reverse side of D.

Flower	You'll Need	Color	See Method	To Make
BABY MUMS	2/3 yd. Regular Rickrack or 1/3 yd. each of two colors	combined or solid—apricot, orange, yellow, canary, wine, red, gold	Interlocking 3B	Coil and tack
POMPON	5 yds. Regular Rickrack	yellow	Interlocking 3C	Tack to 3" circle, then apply to picture.
FORGET-ME-NOTS	1/3 yd. Baby rickrack (makes 2)	yellow, red	Gathering 1C	Cluster and tack.
LEAF CLUSTER	1/3 yd. Jumbo Rickrack (makes 3)	emerald	Leaves 4B	Tack to stems.
STEMS	Tubing or Corded Piping	avocado, emerald	Stems 5C or Stems 5A	Glue or tack.

FALL FLOWERS

Baby Mums
Pompon
Leaf Clusters
Forget-me-nots
Stems

FALL

Flower	You'll Need	Color	See Method	To Make
DAISY	1/3 yd. Jumbo Rickrack / 1/3 yd. Regular Rickrack	white / canary	Gathering 1D / Gathering 1C	Coil and tack in center.
LILAC	2 yd. Regular Rickrack	lavender	Gathering 1A	Tack spirally in cone shape.
HYACINTH	1 yd. Regular Rickrack	pink or lavender	Tacking 2	Make 7 buds for 1 flower. Tack to both sides of stem.
VIOLET	1/3 yd. Regular Rickrack / 1/3 yd. Regular Rickrack (makes 5 double flowers)	lavender / purple	Tacking 2 / Tacking 2	Tack 1 purple thru center of 1 lavender.
FORGET-ME-NOTS	1/3 yd. Baby Rickrack (makes 2 flowers)	white, pink, blue, or yellow	Gathering 1C	Cluster and tack.
LEAVES	1/3 yd. Jumbo Rickrack	emerald	Leaves 4B	Tack to stems.
STEMS	Tubing or Corded Piping	avocado, emerald	Stems 5G / Stems 5A	

SPRING FLOWERS

Daisy
Lilac
Hyacinth
Violet
Forget-me-nots
Leaves
Stems

SUMMER FLOWERS

Marigold
Bachelor Buttons
Zinnia
Daisy
Black Eyed Susan
Forget-me-nots
Leaves
Stems

Flower	You'll Need	Color	See Method	To Make
MARIGOLD	1/2 yd. Regular Rickrack / 1/2 yd. Jumbo Rickrack	canary / canary	Gathering 1A / Gathering 1A	Cluster and tack at center. / Coil and tack around center.
BACHELOR BUTTONS	1/3 yd. Regular Rickrack / 1/3 yd. Regular Rickrack / 1/4 yd. Baby Rickrack	copen, turquoise, yale, or cadet (any two shades combined) / black	Interlocking 3B / Gathering 1C	Coil and tack / Cluster and tack in center.
ZINNIA	2/3 yd. Regular Rickrack / 1/3 yd. Baby Rickrack / 1 yd. Regular Rickrack	gold / canary / rose	Gathering 1B / Gathering 1C / Gathering 1C	Cluster and tack in center. / Use on outside for petals.
DAISY	1/3 yd. Jumbo Rickrack / 1/3 yd. Baby Rickrack	white / canary	Gathering 1D / Gathering 1C	Coil and tack in center.
BLACK EYED SUSAN	1/3 yd. Jumbo Rickrack / 1/3 yd. Baby Rickrack	yellow / seal brown	Gathering 1E / Gathering 1C	Tack petal points. / Cluster and tack in center.
FORGET-ME-NOTS	1/3 yd. Baby Rickrack	white, pink, blue, yellow	Gathering 1C	Cluster and tack.
LEAVES	1/3 yd. Jumbo Rickrack (makes 11)	emerald	Leaves 4A	Tack to stems.
STEMS	Tubing or Corded Piping	avocado, emerald	Stems 5C / Stems 5A	

Flower	You'll Need	Color	See Method	To Make
ROSE BUDS	1/4 yd. Regular Rickrack	pink, old rose, rose, or red	Interlocking 3A	
ROSES	1/2 yd. Regular Rickrack	pink, old rose, rose, or red	Interlocking 3A	
FULL BLOOM ROSE	1 yd. Jumbo Rickrack	rose	Interlocking 3A / Interlocking 3B (1/2 yd. each)	Tack around bud.
CALYX OR FLOWER BASE	1/3 yd. Regular Rickrack (makes 4) or 1/3 yd. Jumbo Rickrack (makes 7)	emerald / emerald	Leaves 4A / Leaves 4A	
STEMS	Baby Rickrack, Tubing or Corded Piping	nile, avocado, emerald	Stems 5B / Stems 5C / Stems 5A	

WINTER FLOWERS

Rose Buds
Roses
Full Bloom Rose
Calyx or Flower Base
Stems

Sheet copper can be used to create a striking mobile for year-round use, or try it as Christmas trims. A mobile of graceful copper figures makes a good gift, too. These shapes, created by Mary Lou Stribling, are fine for beginners.

Copper is easy to handle. Scissors cut light, medium gauges; tin snips cut heavy gauges. Copper is more malleable than tin, yet inexpensive enough for tree baubles, light reflectors. Epoxy glue may be used to join pieces together instead of using solder.

COPPER CREATIONS

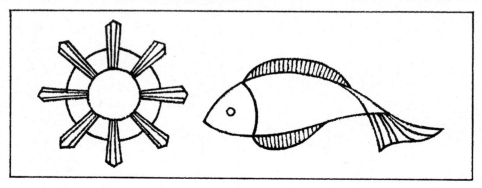

Copper is weatherproof, thus is practical for outdoor use. In unantiqued pieces it takes on a wonderful patina when rained upon. Being fireproof, copper is suitable for candle covers, hurricane lights, and lanterns for outdoor use.

Where sparkle is desired, sheet copper may be used in its bright, polished state. It is antiqued by brushing with a solution made by dissolving a small pea-size lump of liver of sulfur in a quart of hot water, burnishing with fine steel wool in areas to remain bright. Weaker solutions than that described will produce deep gunmetal tones. Solution should be mixed only as needed. It deteriorates within 24 hours.

Sheet copper may be painted with transparent glass lacquers or opaque black airplane enamels. It may be hammered, pierced, or, fringed or tooled.

To copy medium-gauge sheet copper designs shown, trace patterns on copper foil using a dull pencil to indent metal. Cut out with scissors, rub areas to be antiqued with fine steel wool. Antique the designs, following the directions given previously.

 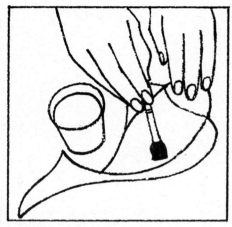 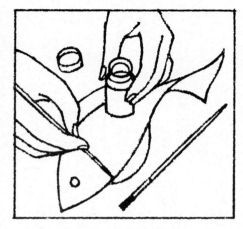

Place the pattern on the copper foil and then trace the lines with a dull pencil so that the metal is indented. If pencil is too sharp, the indenting will not be smooth as with dull pencil.

Cut out shape with scissors, and burnish areas that are to be antiqued with fine steel wool. Apply antiquing solution with a brush until desired color is reached. Rinse with water.

After the shape is completely dry following the clean-water rinse, you are ready to paint the areas to be colored with fast-drying transparent lacquers. "Float" the lacquer on shape.

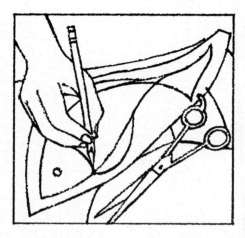 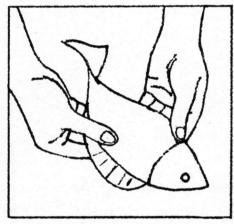 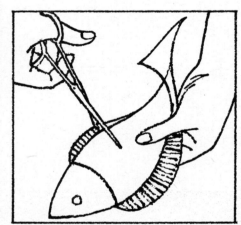

Place lacquered fish on pad of newspaper when dry. Pierce bodies of fish and centers of star circles by tapping with a small chisel and nail with hammer. Work carefully; avoid tearing.

Shape the fish with your hands to round the bodies and give a graceful curve to the tails. Press the star lightly onto newspaper when paint is dry. Leave until the star lies flat.

Cut along the fringed areas with tin snips and shape them as indicated in the picture, opposite page. Glue orange beads or jewels to the eyes of the fish and the center of the star.

Fringe fin of fish by pulling every other strip forward and shaping over fingers. Repeat on back side. Pierce body of fish with a V gauge and small nail. Push V tab to back side to make triangular opening. Slash lines of tail and pull every other strip forward. Paint outlines, eyes, and bodies with transparent orange glass lacquer. On other side, paint same details.

When cutting star, slash lines of rays to inner circle. Pull the outer strips forward slightly, center strip backward in a gentle curve. Fringe between the rays.

Pierce center of the circle with a tiny nail tip. On one side paint rays and center with orange glass lacquer; on the other side, paint the fringed area. Glue beads to the fish eye and the center of the star.

WIRE SCULPTURE

Wire sculptures afford a delightful means of expression for young and old alike. Wire working entails little expense, requires little experience.

For wire sculpture, stock a good supply of 18-gauge wire and 26-gauge wire, a tube of plastic aluminum, and a can of spray enamel paint. Gold, silver, bronze, coppertone, and black paint best simulate the metal tones.

A graceful ostrich, above, is delicately laced. Grazing horse, below, has good lines.

Jungle king, left, has a friendly fierceness that would be appreciated by the young.

Bushy-tail squirrel pauses at play with a tail cocked up along animal's curved back.

Wire frame of most animals is about 6″ long by 5″ to 8″ tall; the swan measures 9″ long by 5″ tall. Make an understructure of the body using a 3-foot length of the heavy-gauge wire. Start at the swan's tail and bend the wire full through body and breast, slim down at the neck and head, return down the "S" curve of neck, bow over back, and fasten wire by wrapping at the tail. Do not cut the wire, as body is made of one continuous, running piece. If wire runs out, you can join on a new length by twisting wire ends around each other.

Repeat swan body following the same lines and shaping as you did the first time. These wires will not show in the finished animal. Wind the same gauge wire around the swan's shell to stabilize it and to round the shape of the swan.

Wings are formed separately in the identical manner as the body. Form a wing structure 5″ long; bend and shape 6 wing-shaped lines within the outline, fasten at the bottom.

Spiral heavier wire to give breadth. Before attaching the sections, it's a good idea to catch wire crossings at random on the body and wings, using bits of fine wire to strengthen, tie, and to round the body. Lace the wings with the heavy wire to the body of the swan, bracing them together. Wind thin wire in any direction over the entire body covering different spots each time to give a lacy effect when you finish.

If, at this point, the wire begins to slip off the form, you then should wind additional strands of wire diagonally over the entire area to take care of this difficulty.

Keep wrapping until the shape is completed.

The octopus is one of the simplest animals to fashion. The first step is to wind a piece of heavy-gauge wire in a 4″ oval; wrap another oval over it at right angles, repeating several times. Then, spiral heavy wire down form you've started until the shape is firm, strong.

The octopus arms are shaped from a continuous piece of wire. To make the arms, fasten the wire at the bottom of the oval and then bend it into a long, scraggly shape. Retrace arm, then hook the wire through the oval. After you've finished this step, it's time to run the wire across the other arm and return to the body of the octopus. Trace each of the arms twice for the best effect. Finally, cover the octopus—including the many arms, with fine wire. Use the 18-gauge wire for this finishing process. First wrap the body and then wrap the arms.

All of the other figures shown here are as easy to fashion as the swan and the octopus, and follow the standard technique. The variations that you might put into the animals you sculpt will just make the finished product more interesting and a more truly personal piece.

To finish the figures, dab plastic aluminum on here and there; it hardens into a rough, soldered metal look.

Then, place the animal on a piece of paper inside a cardboard carton. Spray enamel on the sculpture from about 3 feet away, turning paper to cover all of the surface. The paint coat should be light, even. Let it dry.

Realistic octopus and giraffe with neck coiled high are both simple to fashion, finish.

Creative designs can beautify any room in a home. Even the sewing center, utility room, or other areas in or close to the kitchen respond to the decorative treatment offered by crafts.

A paper mosaic like the ones shown on the opposite page could be made in any shape you need for the space to be filled. Division of the background area should be scaled to fit your specific size.

WELCOME CREATIVE DESIGNS

Pebbles polished smooth by water, starfish, sand dollars, and other souvenirs of the sea are held firm in free-flowing waves of tinted cement, left. To create a mural like this, work out your design lines on tracing paper cut to the exact size. When the lines please you, make a second copy of the basic plan. Then, using one of the patterns, arrange the stones, shells, and other objects to be embedded until you find a design you want. Frame a piece of metal lath with wooden lath. Using the second pattern as a guide, pour in tinted cement, following lines.

Tint cement with water paint. Transfer the stones, shells to design while cement is wet.

The wall mosaic, right, costs little to duplicate, yet is a smart-looking decoration for a paneled wall. Start with a sheet of bristol board purchased at an art shop. Have board cut to exact size. Using a ruler and soft lead pencil, mark off checkerboard design on board. The blocks are then ready to paint; use poster colors black and white. Keep edges sharp with use of masking tape. Next, sketch rest of design on a heavy piece of paper. Using watercolors, paint your design with colors that accent or match your decorating scheme. When the paint is dry, cut painted design into small chips.

Reassemble the chips on your background sheet. It is easier to fit chips together again if a small portion of the design is cut at a time.

When the design is reassembled, glue each of the pieces with transparent glue. Designer of the mosaic wall hanging was Fred Swogger.

The colorful feathers of the hen and rooster are pasted on a wood-grained background in wall hanging, left. These smart chickens had humble beginnings as samples of paint colors, but any of the many smooth-surface papers that come in assorted colors are just as effective in this kind of treatment. First, the design was outlined full-size on piece of butcher's paper. You can use the chickens as a guide, or, use any design of your own.

The next step is to cut the paint chips in angular shapes to fill in the outline of design. The use of closely related colors gives effect of shading to design, adds to the depth.

The background for this wall hanging is a rectangle of thin plywood. Plywood is coated with wood-grained plastic that comes with adhesive-backing. This material is available in housewares sections of markets and department stores.

After the adhesive-backed material is attached, the design is glued down with rubber cement. A wire-hook assembly is used to prepare the wall trim for hanging. Designer was G. Herndon.

MOSAICS OF SEEDS

Seeds, glue, and imagination are all you need to do seed mosaics. Anything you can find in the kitchen cabinets could be used—oats, peas, beans, barley, coffee, spices, uncooked cereals, popcorn, rice. Also, you can consider pebbles, bits of glass, tiny buttons, or shiny coins. Pieces of macaroni, spaghetti are good.

To ready finished piece for hanging, leave it flat for at least 36 hours, then spray with clear plastic. Mount on a second piece of plywood that is stained.

To start seed mosaic, you'll need soft pencil, tracing paper, plywood board, transparent glue, clear shellac, toothpicks, palette knife, assorted seeds.

Plan your picture in detail on tracing paper, writing in colors and materials planned for each area. Color back of the paper, lay on plywood, and then retrace the design. Now you're ready for the seeds.

After outlining important details, fill in the background areas—a small section at time. Try for exciting contrast in color, texture. Spread layer of glue with palette knife and follow with a generous covering of tea, coffee, or herbs of your choice. Use the knife edge to make lines clean and distinct.

Press seeds down with fingers and let set. Fill in gaps.

Begin filling in design, working from the edges to center. Cover penciled lines with glue and set larger seeds with your tweezers. Use a knife to push small seeds.

Seeds that have a definite design or shape, such as kidney beans, should face in the same direction. Try macaroni or spaghetti sticks for flower stems, spacers. Use corn or beans for important lines.

CEMENT PAINTING

Only simple and easy-to-obtain materials are necessary to follow the concrete-painting method that was developed by Architect Roy Binkley. Most of the materials can be purchased at your local lumber store. The artists' oil colors are available in any art-supply store, stationery store.

The first step is to make a firm framework for the wet concrete. Nail a piece of metal lath to a rectangle or square of ½-inch plywood. This should be the size you want for finished painting, exclusive of framing. Next, add frame by nailing lengths of wood lath around edges of plywood.

Follow the instructions given at the right for pouring of the cement, finishing of the design.

After you've finished, and the cement painting is dry, you're ready to paint. For a quiet, subtle effect, use paint sparingly on background.

Spread concrete in shallow tray formed by metal lath and plywood. After mixing water with premixed sand concrete, fill frame to depth of about ¾ of inch. Use an ordinary garden trowel to smooth the wet concrete and work it into the metal lath.

When the concrete is level and smooth, but still wet, start forming the design. Old spoons, piece of wood, or regular modeling tools can be used for this work. Work out design on paper first, use as a guide when you start on the concrete. To vary effect, embed a few pebbles or shells into picture.

MOSAICS

There's no special secret to mastering mosaics, one of the most rewarding and popular of crafts. Here are 12 fresh designs to inspire you to create a design of your own. Start with a smaller project. Then the large pieces will become easier. Some of the designs are planned for personal use; others are ideal for use in your own home or as gifts. Once you master the craft, you'll find the work goes quickly.

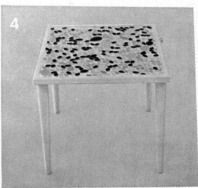

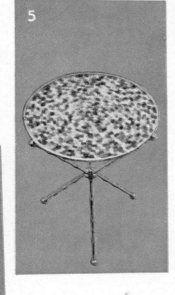

Mosaic work, an ancient art now revived, gains its modern appearance with old techniques. It offers beauty and practicality, plus unlimited original ideas. Basic mosaic tiles come in porcelain, marble, ceramics, glass. **Materials:** In addition to tiles, you will need cutter, glue, and grout cement—items found in hobby or hardware stores. Unfinished plywood gives a sturdy backing; or framed, double-strength glass is used when a transparent effect is desired. To cut the tile, insert 1/8 inch into cutting blade and squeeze gently. It's a good idea to use safety goggles. **Techniques:** To start, lay tiles in design you want on heavy paper cut to size. Then transfer tiles, one by one, from paper to your project.

Apply small bits of adhesive to base itself or to the individual tiles. Press to adhere. Let design set overnight before grouting. To color grouting, mix it with dry pigment first, then add water according to package directions. With gloved hand, spread mixture; press into crevices. Wipe off excess after five minutes. Let it stand 10 hours; wash thoroughly with sponge to finish and clean it.

• Here are 12 mosaics to try:
1. Primitive pussy-cat picture is set into a pine frame. Hang singly or in pairs. Look in art books, embroidery books, magazines for patterns and designs.
2. This tabletop looks complicated, but takes only patience.

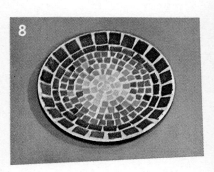

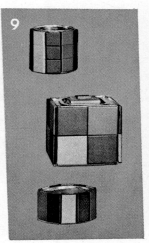

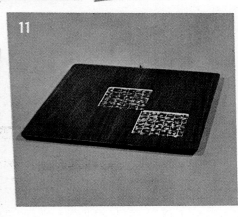

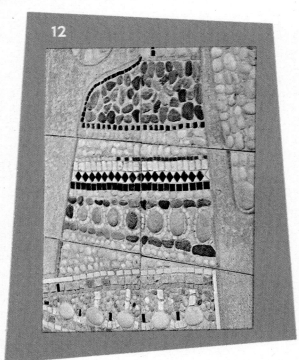

3. For an effective desk accessory, ceramic tile is set into recessed lid of wooden box.
4. Group ceramic pieces at random in tinted cement. Table is painted to match cement.
5. On a glass-topped table, multicolored tile is left ungrouted for light to filter through.
6. Venetian glass relish tray is an easy-to-make gift item.
7. Soft clay tiles, broken and set in door pulls, add color to cabinets and drawers.
8. Handsome masculine ashtray was once a baking pan.
9. Unglazed tiles transform tin cans into desk accessories.
10. Glazed ceramics make fine drawer pulls.
11. Trim a cheese board with colorful mosaics.
12. Exposed pebbles give a textured look. For additional details, see page 166.

PAPER TRAYS

Papier-mache mementos are old in origin, placing the value of earlier designs in the category of collector's pieces.

Designer Ann Joselyn makes and gives her own creations—modern-day treasures. If you adapt this idea, you can style, color, and size your pieces to suit a specific person you have in mind.

You can use adhesive-backed papers, flower magazines, foreign stamps, foil candy wrappers, gold paper medallions, inexpensive prints as part of a design. After decoration has been applied, coat entire tray with nontoxic, waterproof, transparent spray. This surfacing will give a permanence to tray and design with its hard finish. Spray makes it possible to wipe tray clean after use.

Two small trays fit inside larger one. Spray-paint all three with flat black and edge with gilt. Decorate base with gold and turquoise mosaic pattern paper. This paper is adhesive-backed plastic. Make several sets of these to give for gifts.

The basic tray forms are pulp paper liners used to contain fruits and meats in the grocery store. When you are making your collection, be sure to obtain two of every size. You will glue two together for each section, making a more rigid form. Some smaller trays fit inside a larger size, making into handsome sets for serving snacks. Others will serve various other purposes.

Other materials you will need include dry, ground gesso which dries to a hard, plaster-like finish. Follow directions for mixing, then apply three coats of gesso to trays that have been glued together. When gesso is dry, the tray becomes rigid and is ready to be smoothed with sandpaper. Tray is now prepared for decorating. Apply fancy paper, the stamps, other trims. Spray to finish.

Rose-centered perfume tray was spray-painted white and edged with gilt. Select from nursery catalog a picture of a rose. Before gluing down, cut block of red paper and glue underneath rose blossom; glue similar block of green under the stem. This adds balance.

Glue rose on, centering over the color blocks. Finish with nontoxic, waterproof, transparent spray.

After you are done, group perfume bottles here and there so the rose design shows. If you prefer, another type of flower cut from nursery catalog could be adapted just as effectively.

Wall trims are simple to make, following the decorated tray directions. A young artist would like to have a good art print like this given a permanent treatment with gesso, transparent spray.

To reproduce this mounting, spray a tray jet green, a color that harmonizes well with picture. Accent the edge with a band of gilt to give a more dimensional feeling to recessed print.

Children's art work would be fun to exhibit like this. For it, choose gay color for the tray. They will last for years when treated with plastic spray. They can be dusted, wiped with sponge.

Plastic describes many man-made materials that look alike but are very different in composition. Some are unusable by home craftsmen because they are dangerous or require elaborate mechanical treatment. There is one particular form of thermoplastic that is nontoxic and is safe to use at home. As you can see by the decorative and useful things shown, it has endless possibilities as a craft material.

All you need for a laboratory is plenty of space to work and a regular kitchen oven with a thermostat, to insure a constant temperature of 375°. You'll need plastic pellets, smooth foil pans, copper wire, colored chalk, colored papers, pebbles, and glass nuggets. Shown below are just a few of the many ways you can use pellets to get a variety in texture, shapes.

PLASTICS IN THE OVEN

Plastic pellets look like clear little crystal beads. Depending on how long they're heated in a 375° oven (from 15 to 45 minutes), they can be softened to barely adhere together or melted to form a nubby or even flat surface.

Do not broil plastic. Do not worry about nontoxic odor given off during baking.

The size of the piece you make is limited only by the size of your oven and molds. Thickness can be varied. It is reworkable. Two pieces can be fused together by letting the edges touch.

Level the pellets before placing them in the oven. To avoid a sharp edge, bevel away from edge with a pancake turner. Plastic makes crackling noise as it cools.

Molds. Plastic can be put in thin, metal cake pans or on baking sheets. Or you can use metal salad molds, tin sandbox toys, cookie cutters. Even molds you form of heavy aluminum foil, disposable foil pans that have embossing smoothed out with a hot iron can be used. Avoid ring molds. Avoid glass dishes.

The hot plastic will be soft and malleable when taken from oven. If it has been softened over foil, and you work quickly with gloves, it can be bent or shaped. File off any sharp edges.

Frames. Plastic will adhere to wood, so unpainted picture frames, embroidery hoops or strips of wood nailed together can be used as permanent frames. Plastic is melted directly into frames, with a metal base underneath. Wood will darken somewhat in oven. Frames should be weighted during cooling.

Almost anything, pebbles, foil, shells, leaves, seeds, yarn, can be embedded. Cover burnable items on both sides with complete layer plastic.

Colorants. You can dye pellets by using colored chalk. Into enameled pan, grate ½ inch chalk stick for each cup of pellets. Add water to cover. Bring to boil, stirring often until nearly dry. Put pellets on pad of newspaper and spread out. Let dry.

Partially melted pieces can be painted with special enamels for plastics. It does not change color when heated. It's opaque at full strength.

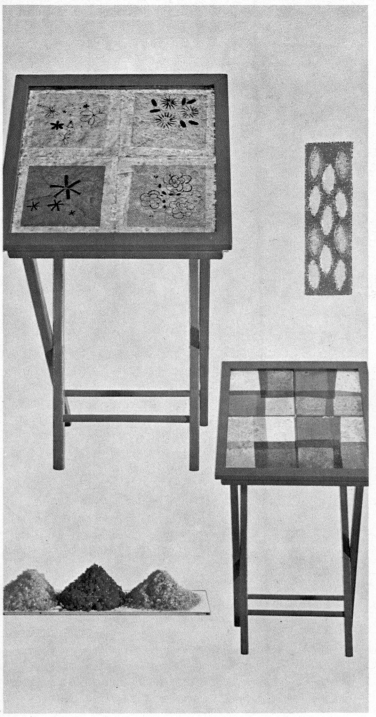

Each tabletop was made of four pieces of plastic molded in 7-inch-square pans. Finished pieces were placed in unpainted wood frames and more pellets were added at the joints. Then, entire assembly was reheated to fuse it together. Campstool legs complete tables. Legs and frames were painted before the final assembly.

The hanging panel was made of clear molded ovals arranged in a loaf pan. The ovals were surrounded with brilliant pellets, then fused.

Colored tissue paper produces translucent effects when used as part of the design. Opaque papers make silhouettes. The artwork can be done on tissue with chalk, black India ink, or liquid watercolors before embedding. Papers should be protected by complete layer of pellets about 3/16-inch thick, both under and over them, to prevent burning during time in oven. Nonflammable materials don't need covering.

Room divider was molded in two sizes of flat disposable pans. Silhouettes were cut from gold foil wallpaper and embedded in pellets that had been previously dyed in shades of green. Both of the sides had additional pellets fused on lightly for texture. Screw eyes were heated and then inserted to hold the hanging chains. All melted pieces will have little bubbles in them like Venetian glass. It's a good idea to look in the oven every ten minutes while a piece is baking to check on the progress.

Thin sheet aluminum, sold in hardware stores, can be used for forming a piece too big for a pan. Or use a makeshift base contrived by completely covering corrugated paper with foil. This tends to give off a disagreeable odor if heated too long. Do not use fiberboard in the oven—it is toxic. Scraps of fiberglass paneling such as that sold for screens and windows can be used. Fiberglass is a thermosetting plastic and does not adhere to thermoplastic pellets.

NATURE CRAFT

When collected treasures of nature become part of his room decor, a child's interest is encouraged. Make it possible to organize and display his collection so he can enjoy it.

For the beginning collector, glue the "finds" to a series of painted display panels. Drill holes in upper corners, allowing the panels to be hung.

For the more advanced collector, more complicated crafts are in order. Gourds already resemble a bowl or dipper, thus are easy to fashion into finished shapes. Drawer pulls can be made from nuts or seeds; hot dish holders make use of several pocketfuls of stones. Fern in placemat was dried, mounted onto a piece of hardboard. Flowers, embedded in casting resin, make fine paperweights.

All children are collectors. Their pockets bulge with rocks, leaves, bugs, or sunflower seeds. They bring home those things that attract their attention. And what then? Too often, from pocket, to box, to wastebasket! And a disappointed child discovers that his hoardings have been discarded. **Besides the panels** shown above, other collections may be kept in felt-lined cigar boxes. With the lids removed, they become shadow boxes for insects, shells, or rocks. They can be attached to the wall or room divider.

A panel of fiberboard allows for pinning; this may be preferable for collections which might need to be removed (cocoons or a chrysalis that will hatch). By covering the board with colored fabric, or painting it in different colors, it is easy to display separate collections on the single panel of fiberboard.

Exhibiting the collections allows a child to keep learning, to keep looking, and perhaps most important, suggests that adults, too, value those pursuits.

As a child becomes more aware of the details in Nature, he becomes more discriminating. Thus, he looks at many shells, and selects special ones—perhaps for their color or shapes. Later on he will select according to types or for variety. But in the beginning, his appetite is various and refreshingly vigorous.

A butterfly is no longer just a butterfly, but it turns into a monarch, or a viceroy, or a swallowtail, attracted to certain of the plants, with a recognizable caterpillar and a rare and distinctive chrysalis to look for.

Collections need not always be made in terms of like objects. A child with a great fondness for orange may collect all things of that color—shells, butterflies, ladybugs, seeds, and flowers.

Or perhaps a child is fascinated by Nature's "containers"—seedpods, wasp nests (unoccupied), and cocoons.

Collections of like objects often grow into more lasting interests—the older child may wish to identify and classify his wild flowers, feathers, leaves, bugs, butterflies and moths.

An interest in bugs or in rocks isn't limited to the child who may wish to grow up to be a professional entomologist or a geologist—it's a way of learning all about the world, the way things grow, the way they are formed, and the way they've been put to use.

Primitive societies used natural forms for many of their tools, utensils, ornaments. Our children can still make many of these same "discoveries." Naturally inventive and creative, they find that the natural forms suggest many uses. And there is an added pleasure when a child sees them put to use at home.

Pictured below are several very usable articles—all made from the simplest, most available materials we could think of. Let your youngster try these ideas first, then see what he can come up with by using his own imagination and natural creativeness.

Hot dish holder from pebbles: The first step is to select stones to be used. Then, arrange them on firm plywood board, checking to be sure they are at least

fairly uniform in size and shape to provide an even surface for the dish holder.

When arranged so that you can determine how large an area can be covered, trace a line around this and saw the plywood. Let the shapes of the stones determine the wood shape. Or, you can cut a circular or a rectangular form.

Next, glue stones with an epoxy according to directions on the package. Cover the bottom of the plywood holder with a piece of felt to prevent scratching of the table surface during use. Plywood can be painted or stained.

Drawer pulls: Drawer fronts provide a logical and practical means of showing and using prize collections. All of the pulls will become conversation pieces in a home. These three pulls suggest a few of the many possibilities.

sand them, attach flowers, add finished coat of plastic, shellac, or varnish. The finished disk is then attached to a long screw or to a ready-made drapery holder. Carefully drill holes in backs and epoxy the screw heads into the holes.

Gourd scoops: To dry, gourds must be left on the vine until they are fully ripened. Then, in picking, be sure to leave a portion of the stem on the gourd. It takes one or two months to dry them thoroughly.

After the gourds are completely dry, select ones with especially nice shapes. For each gourd, cut an opening with a coping saw or a sharp knife. Sand the edges until they are smooth. Sand lightly on the inside and paint with enamel or latex if you want color

on the inside. Bowl, shown at the left in photograph, was scalloped with a half-round file. Decorative holes were drilled at ends of scallops. Other scoop was left in natural shape, without trim. .

Fern placemat: Placemat is cut from one-eighth-inch hardboard (measures 13 by 30 inches). The edges are rounded slightly to give a finished look. Ferns and leaves are pressed between the pages of a large book. When thoroughly dried (this may take days or even weeks), they are ready for mounting. Undercoat and paint the mat any color that you desire. Or, as was done with one shown, paint white and then adhere a layer of colored tissue.

The next step is to attach ferns and leaves using a water-base plastic glue—any white glue will work.

The drawer pulls shown at the bottom in the photograph consist of large wooden knobs which are covered with collections of seeds. One is centered with nut; the other with a light pebble. Use any clear-drying white glue to fashion pulls of this type.

In the center, nuts are glued directly to the wood of the drawer front. White glue was used in process.

On the upper drawer, wood disks, cut from a log, then sanded smooth and shellacked, are cemented to concave metal pulls with white glue. Metal pulls of this type come in many sizes, a variety of colors.

Wood disk curtain pulls: Slices are cut crosswise from small wooden log (not green wood). These are then sanded smooth. Pressed dried flowers are attached with white glue. Liquid plastic, shellac, or varnish goes over all to protect the flowers and to keep wood from soiling when it is handled.

Drill a hole in the wood edge, then insert a curtain cord or a ribbon to complete the pull. This ribbon or cord can be compressed into the hole and then glued. Or, tie a knot at back of the hole to hold. A dot of glue at the edges will be helpful, too.

Drapery holder: Disks of wood are made the same as the curtain pulls above. Start with slices of wood—

Use the glue generously to fill in the spaces around the stems. When it's dry, spray or paint with liquid plastic. Two or three coats of plastic may be necessary to make the placemat completely washable.

Paperweights: New casting resins make it simple to embed bugs, seeds, or flowers into forms for use as paperweights. Use Christmas balls as molds. Remove metal hanger; break larger opening in balls. Rest—open side up—in an egg carton for support.

Plastic embedding resin is mixed according to the package directions and poured into the mold. When the first layer is still tacky, place tiny sprig of evergreen or flower petals in the ball. When the resin dries, add a second layer to completely cover the petals or evergreen or other trims that you used.

When this dries, peel away the ball. If you use a silver-lined ball, some of the silvering may stick. Remove this with a cloth dipped in acetone.

Colored fabric or paper may be placed under any of the paperweights, allowing the color to show through the resin. Or the bottom edge may be sanded smooth—this gives a frosted effect to the paperweight.

Make several of these to give as gifts at holiday time or use them as favors at a special party.

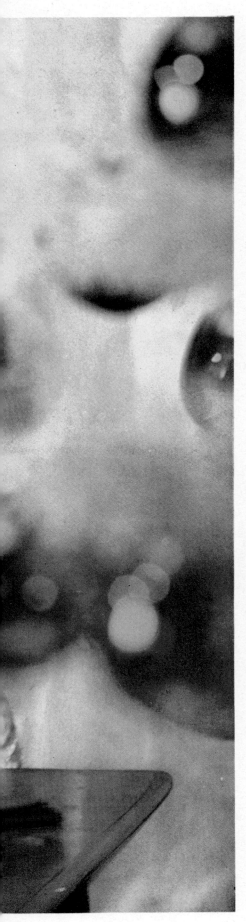

ROPE TRICK

Woolly lion is made of rope, hemp, twine, and burlap—it looks like an expensive import rather than a home-crafted article. The method is simple, you just unwind one strand from each piece of rope and insert two lengths of florist wire. Then wind the strands with the wire back into place. You can use the same technique to make figures of rope or make other animals. At holiday time, try a complete creche scene; the rope figures go well with natural-looking manger and straw. You'll treasure it for years.

For the rope lion, you'll need the following supplies: 12 inches of 1½-inch rope, 24 inches of ½-inch rope, 10 inches of ⅜-inch rope, 2 yards of Manila twine, a tiny scrap of green and of red felt, 6 pieces of 18-inch long florist wire. Now you're ready to start the rope trick!

To make the body, cut the 24-inch piece of rope in half and then wire it. Tie the ends with a small length of florist wire.

Lay two leg pieces flat. Add the 1½-inch rope and the ⅜-inch rope and wind all of the pieces together for about one inch. Continue wrapping for about three more inches and fasten with a knot.

You will have 8 inches left for neck and head. Unwind the three strands and follow sketches to make the head. Rope is combed out for mane around the head.

When adding wire to the rope, be sure to use same length of florist wire as rope. Replace strand over the wire. The rope is then wired or glued into the groove.

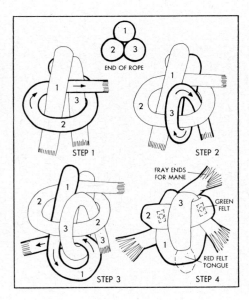

YOU'RE THE DESIGNER

Designing and printing your own greetings and note paper is a satisfying craft; it'll hold your interest for years and will make all of your personal correspondence individual.

W. E. Ross, a veteran in many arts, shares some proven methods of designing and printing. They vary from the age-old technique of fish prints that's complete with a modern adaptation, to simple stencil method. Either will give you enjoyment, interesting results.

Unique technique starts with a fiberboard panel. Sand and paint card-size, fiberboard panel. Draw the design with waterproof black ink; trail cement evenly on dried ink line. Next, spread coating of thinned printer's ink or artist's oil colors over a sheet of glass; roll an inexpensive printer's roller across. Hold Japanese paper firmly on panel, run inked roller over. Ink ball prints on the paper by patting.

The Japanese fish print still is an effective method of printing, although the technique itself is ancient.

Clean up a freshly caught fish and pin to board.

While the fish still is wet, mold thin rice paper over it. Work quickly.

Dab paper with folded pads of cloth dampened in watercolor paints or in poster paints, using one pad for each of the colors.

A more modern version replaces fish with clay. Obtain 5 pounds of clay, roll out ½ inch thick. When hard, trace on pattern. Carve from printing areas.

Tint transfers from clay and fiberboard by using one or more stencils as guides. For each change of color, a piece of stencil paper goes over the card. Trace the patterns. Three color changes create a pleasing blend; haphazard use will mar design.
Place stencil pattern on a sheet of glass and cut along lines with sharp knife or the corner of a single-edged razor blade. Lay the stencil over card and dab or stipple on watercolor paints or colored inks using small sponge for dabbing.
Though color adds vitality, some designs have good enough lines to look strong in black and white.

If using color stencils, take care when removing them. Lift off vertically or wet paints will smear and lines of the card will become fuzzy or even blurred.

Of the two processes, the clay mold reproductions have sharper lines, especially if the paper is pressed onto mold with damp cloth to show design in relief. These clay molds are quite fragile and, unless fired in a kiln, are subject to breakage.

Clay molds can be inked directly and the dampened paper laid on. Apply even pressure with un-inked roller, ink ball, or the back of a large-bowled spoon.

Silk-screen art is a process of stenciling by forcing ink through a silk mesh. Only a few seconds are required to complete one card or one print. You can use the same silk screen over and over again, printing image after image. Try it for a holiday greeting, or for stationery.

SILK SCREEN

Silk screening is a simple process in which film, covering design or background, is made to adhere to a silk screen. The pattern is printed in one stroke by pulling ink down a framed, hinged screen with a rubber-edged tool called a squeegee.

Illustrated below are the materials you need to try one of the simple processes you can follow. A second process, negative printing, also requires minimum materials, little effort. Select either process—you will have fun working with silk screens.

An easy way to use a silk screen is illustrated above. This is called the Tusche Resist Method in which you paint a design upon the silk screen with tusche, a very heavy paint, then cover the entire screen with glue resist. The tusche is removed from the screen by washing with turpentine or kerosene, resulting in open spaces for the printing. The glue stops color from passing through the screen to the background. This method is adequate for a casual effect; it is a natural for the freehand artist since applying tusche is quite a bit like painting a picture.

The silk screen, your first need, is available in hobby stores as are all other materials mentioned. When you have all the supplies, the first step is to lay cardboard beneath the screen to keep the wood panel clean. Draw design on sheet of paper size of your card or paper and place on cardboard. Close screen over and adjust paper until design is centered. Place register marks on cardboard so you can line up the corners or sides of the succeeding papers.

Apply tusche directly upon the screen—

keep design in position beneath the screen to trace over. Brush tusche on pattern to be printed with a small-size, sable lettering brush. Practice on paper to get the feel of the amount of the tusche wanted on the brush.

Though the tusche is so heavy it scarcely hardens, brace frame open and allow to remain in this position for 30 minutes so tusche will set. While frame is still open apply warmed glue, diluted about one half with water, to all areas you don't want printed.

Scrape glue evenly across the entire surface of screen, including parts done with tusche, with the straight edge of a cardboard. Make sure the screen is completely covered; scrape off excess. Allow about a half-hour to dry; put on a thin second coat and let it dry for an hour.

Remove glue-covered tusche by

scrubbing screen briskly with cloth soaked in turpentine, kerosene, or a recommended solvent. Remember precautions when working with inflammable solutions. Wipe entire screen clean with a dry cloth.

The reverse of this process is called Negative Printing. Again lay drawing under screen and trace it with a tiny brush dipped in glue. Add a few drops of tempera paint to glue so you can see it better on screen. The outside edge, and any pattern detail you want seen, must be completely sealed off with glue so paint will not seep through. In this printing, the color will print in the areas you have not covered with glue—this usually includes the background.

Prepare ink for printing by mixing it half and half with transparent base. Water soluble paints cannot be used where there is glue resist as they would dissolve it. Pour ink along upper inside of screen in line above pattern. Hold squeegee at a 45-degree angle inside the screen and with one stroke draw the solution down slowly and evenly. Repeat ink treatment for each of cards.

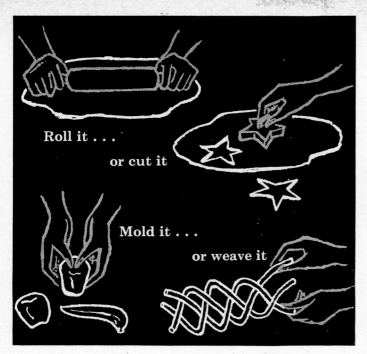

Roll it . . .

or cut it

Mold it . . .

or weave it

MODELING GOOP

Magic modeling goop is a delightful mixture that you can roll, cut, mold, or weave. It leaves no mess on hands, clothes, furniture, thus it's ideal for even the youngest members of the family. You can give the finished pieces a ceramic look by adding three coats of shellac. Let each of the coats dry thoroughly.

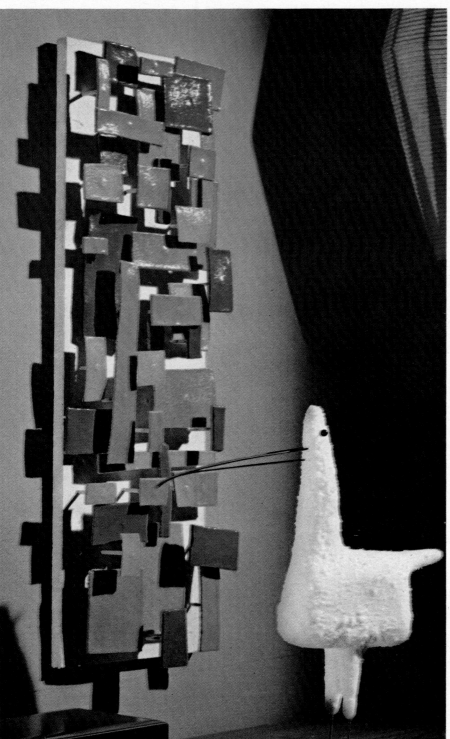

The recipe for the modeling goop is simple. Mix 2 cups of table salt and ⅔ cup water in a saucepan. Stir until mixture is well heated, or about 3 to 4 minutes. Remove from heat and add 1 cup cornstarch which has been mixed with ½ cup cold water. Stir quickly to mix.

The mixture should be the consistency of stiff dough. If the mixture does not turn this thick, place over low heat, stir about 1 minute until the desirable smooth pliable mass is formed.

You can leave the mixture natural white, or you can divide it into portions and add regular food colors till the desired brilliance and color are achieved. Or, the modeled objects may be decorated or painted when dry to give surface color.

The mix can be kept indefinitely if wrapped in a clear plastic wrap or foil. The recipe makes 1¾ pound of the modeling goop. No refrigeration is necessary.

To dry goop, let the modeled objects dry, harden at room temperatures for approximately 36 hours, depending upon the thickness of the objects. Place models on a wire rack or screen to allow air to move freely around all surfaces. Objects with large mass of modeling goop should be pierced by a pencil when moist to allow interiors to dry.

You can make a wide variety of accessories for your home, using a recipe of modeling goop. Wall plaque is formed with squares of dried mix pegged into fiberboard. A bird is shaped around plastic-foam.

You don't need a lot of time to start working on a craft. A quiet evening is ideal for trying your hand at some of the simpler projects. Or, set aside a few hours on a weekend. Many crafts can be mastered in a hurry, giving results that will amaze you. Other craft forms are a little more complicated and require a slow development of skill. But, even the first learning stages can be fun.

Block printing holds a time-honored place in the craft field. One of the easiest variations of block-printing method, shown at left, promises to gain new friends for this activity. Modern block prints are taken from plastic foam, the materials are easy to obtain, and results are handsome.

To try this method of block printing, you'll need a flat rectangle of plastic foam, a sharp knife, a paint tray and roller, heavy, textured paper, water-base paint.

Plan your design first, scaling it to fit the piece of plastic foam. A design with simple lines works effectively. Using a straight pin, lightly scratch the design on foam surface. Take a sharp knife and make deep V cuts to outline design.

Then, roll water-base paint on the foam, making sure to cover evenly. Spread a sheet of heavy paper over the block and rub it with your hands, starting at the center and working toward the edges.

Carefully pull the paper up; hold just by the margins. Let dry. You may want to pull several prints to get the best design pattern.

CRAFTS YOU CAN MASTER

Photograms make it easy to be artistic. They can magically transform everyday objects into striking pictures.

Blueprint paper is the easiest material to use for this unusual craft. The first step is to lay the paper on small piece of plywood, arrange objects on it, then cover the paper and objects with a piece of glass to keep them flat and in place during the important exposure period.

Expose to sunlight for about 1 minute or to artificial light for 5 to 10 minutes. After this step is finished it is time to wash the print in water. Next, dip it in hydrogen peroxide to stop the developing action. Hang the prints to dry, using pinch-type clothespins.

Use the finished prints for dust jackets for books, or you can frame them for use in a living area, family room.

By nature, crafts have one main characteristic in common —they allow you to work with your hands as well as your mind. This gives you an active kind of satisfaction. Also, you will find that many of the tricks and techniques that are learned for one craft can be applied to a new art with no difficulty. Your skill and confidence will grow naturally as you try working with the many crafts and arts.

Wood tape scraps shape into interesting mosaics, under the direction of John and Janet Trimmis. The color variation is wide, lets strong contrasts emerge. The pale blonde tones stand out against the deep mahoganies and the darkest of the walnut-toned pieces.

To start on a wood mosaic you should draw your design on a section of tempered hardboard. Chalk or a soft lead pencil will mark hardboard. You'll need adhesive-backed wood edging tape in many finishes. Using scissors, cut the scraps of the edging tape to mosaic-like pieces to fit design.

Fill background—all hardboard should be covered. Iron the tape onto hardboard with an electric iron. When your wood mosaic is complete, you can apply a coat of clear shellac to make finish durable and easy to keep clean.

Abstractions with ease. Whoever heard of oilcan paintings? No one until now! But we think you'll enjoy this speedy, spontaneous, and uninhibited way to paint. Even your most undirected pieces usually turn out to be happy accidents. One way or another, you have the fun connected with creating.

From line drawing to flashy abstracts, effects unlike any other form of painting are created by blowing through the tube and drizzling color onto paper. School-age children especially love this free, unpredictable type of action painting.

The first step is to drill a hole in any size of machine oilcan, solder in a 1-inch length of 1/8-inch copper tubing, then attach a 2-foot length of flexible rubber or plastic tubing. Fill the can 2/3 full of tempera, casein, watercolor, or inexpensive enamel. (Children should use only nontoxic poster paints!)

The next step is to blow through the tube, directing paint with the spout. Vary the lines in size and shape by slowing your hand movement, blowing harder, and applying from different heights. It's a good idea to have papers on your work surface unless it is easily washed to prevent damage from splatters.

Begin by painting on paper and poster boards. For the paintings you want to keep, use wallboard, decorator's canvas pasted to plywood, artists' canvas, or hardboard—all more durable than paper.

You'll be amazed at the many effects you can create —for example, by two wet colors falling one on another, or by standing and splashing the paint on a floor canvas. Or, if you want a dramatic one-color look, use only black paint on a white surface. You can frame your best for a personal art collection.

FUN CRAFTS

Furniture for Lilliputian living. You can furnish a doll house with designs so realistic they'd go over big in Lilliput—and, what's more important, the little girl in your family will be truly delighted.

Miniature reproduction of fine furniture is a craft you'll never stop developing once you start. As a beginning, you'll probably find the simple lines of contemporary furniture easier to follow. Next, you'll want to copy models from books on the many various styles of furniture design, or create your own designs. Use the convenient scale of 1 inch equals 1 foot when you are copying furniture or creating your own. The scale is large enough to make working easy.

These miniature Early American secretaries, only a foot high, were made from light balsa wood. This simple material is available in most crafts, hobby shops. It's easy to cut and glue, and you can vary the shapes of individual pieces without difficulty. To work with balsa wood, you need only a single-edge razor blade or hobby knife, and a water-soluble glue for the assembly.

The first step is to select the chest, table, chair, or a sofa that you'd like to reproduce as scaled-down furniture. Use a ruler to scale dimensions of the piece you've selected. Then, blueprint your selection. Get each piece drawn on paper. For the best results, try the wood pieces of furniture first, then go on to the more complicated upholstered miniatures. For example, a simple dining chair or a table is easier to fashion than a sofa.

To upholster these tiny creations, use adhesive-backed moleskin (available in drugstores and food markets) or cotton for padding. This padding is then covered by gluing brightly colored fabric scraps over it. If you wish, you can hem the fabric scraps before gluing, or glue in a hem on raw edges. Scraps of brocade, taffeta, small-patterned prints are especially rich and give a real upholstered look. Little remnants of brightly-colored printed papers make effective liners for chest shelves, or use them to cover the tops of tables.

Use an artist's paintbrush to apply the wood stains, a fingernail-polish brush to add details such as painted pulls and handles. Or, antique furniture by trimming it with gold and white.

MEN WHO CREATE WITH WOOD

When Spring seems a long stretch of the calendar, there's nothing like the feeling of accomplishment you get from the old craft of working with wood. It's a durable kind of craft, low in cost, and the products are welcome in your home or in gift packages. You can create a toymaker's workshop, or team wood and sand.

One unusual way of working with wood was developed by Jack Denst of Chicago. He makes sand castings that use pieces of nicely shaped driftwood as an important part of the design.

Besides the wood he finds himself, Jack's good friends send him pieces found on the Pacific coast, in Florida, and along various river banks across the country. To make a casting, he smoothes damp sand on his sand table, shown at right, banking it up to form the outline of his mold. He arranges the pieces of wood and textures the sand around them with a trowel. Then he mixes the sand, water, and casting plaster and pours it over the wood and the background. Pebbles, other items from the water's edge help make the designs interesting.

You can make toyland treasures from wooden blocks. Toymaking, a craft with the magical quality of childhood, can be a simple, a satisfying process when you put your workshop to use for the joy of your youngsters.

Remember the spool-and-rubber band convoys you produced as a boy? The same principle motorizes these little wooden cars, which make safe and uncomplicated toys that are ideal for any boy.

These are made from two-inch blocks of select grade white pine that were shaped with a band saw. The bodies are a solid piece of wood, with holes for metal tubing axles and for 1/8-inch dowel steering rods. A slice of 3/4-inch dowel is the steering wheel for each of the cars.

One of the first steps is to force metal tubing into wheels and through body for axles. Drill body holes slightly larger in diameter than the wheel openings for the best operation.

For a rear-wheel "motor," you can wind a large rubber band around a 3-inch length of 1/8-inch dowel. Draw the band through a small dowel round (which serves as a hub), then through the axle and secure to a small nail on the opposite wheel. Then, lubricate the "hub" with soap. After you have done this, you're ready to wind stick, watch them roll.

Finish the cars by sanding. Also, you can paint cars if you wish. Use nontoxic paint for any toys used by children. Paint all one color, or use several colors.

While you have wood at hand, cut a series of blocks like those pictured in foreground. They comprise a fraction board, to teach arithmetic. The blocks should be designated 1, 1/2, 1/4, 1/8, or can be colored to indicate divisions. Cut them to fit a simple frame.

UNUSUAL
CRAFTS

You can customize tables or door mats for your home by following these craft techniques. Spatter craft is foolproof and fabulous way to finish a piece of furniture. Even if you've never lifted a paintbrush, you can achieve beautiful results on tables, counter tops, serving trays. Or, finish a table with a gold top at the price of paper; add a whimsical touch to ordinary door mat.

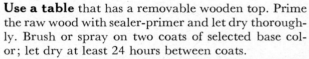

Use a table that has a removable wooden top. Prime the raw wood with sealer-primer and let dry thoroughly. Brush or spray on two coats of selected base color; let dry at least 24 hours between coats.

Apply first spatter coat by tapping *side* of brush held in one hand against a stick held in the other. Thin enough so paint spreads well and leaves a little-raised surface. Use a stiff-bristled brush.

The higher one works while spattering, the larger the paint spreads. If large droplets are desired, about half-dollar size, hold brush about 3 to 6 inches away. Next, add second and third spatter colors that have been thinned down, using a clean brush for each. Let each coat dry before adding another. Three gold metallic colors were applied to this table after using shades of red, orange, and crimson on a magenta base.
When dry, rub lightly with emery paper. Wipe clear with clean cloth before you apply plastic varnish. A light coat of wax gives a mirrorlike finish. Spatter craft works with either lacquer or enamel paints.

It's wise to practice first on an old board before you start a prized piece of furniture. Work with a drop cloth under board to prevent unwanted paint spatters.

The **first step** of gold-topped table is to pretreat the paper. Then tear the uneven shapes, then cover background as explained in the directions below.

You can customize your coco fiber door mat with your monogram, street number, or a cheerful design. Your guests will appreciate this welcome.

Start by creating your own design on paper the size of your door mat—use brown wrapping paper, or newspaper if you have a heavy marking pencil. Cut a thin corrugated or stencil cardboard to mat size and trace on the chosen design. Cut along all the lines with scissors or sharp knife. Cover floor with a newspaper to catch drifting paint spray, then assemble pieces of stencil on mat.

Remove pieces to be painted same color and spray-paint with flat enamel. Replace stencil over painted surface; uncover and paint each different color.

Gold foil collage is easy to create. To begin it, wrinkle gold paper-backed foil then flatten an area and spray with a quick-drying enamel. Moisten a cloth with turpentine to rub paint over the foil. Repeat until all the foil is covered with paint. Next, tear the foil into random shapes. You'll need to have one and a half times the area to be covered with the finished collage. This percentage gives a good finished look.

Have a brush, white glue, and sponge ready for use. Select foil pieces at random; glue to the surface of the table. The overlapped shapes produce a unique dark and light pattern.

Stain raw white edges of the foil paper with burnt sienna oil color thinned in turpentine. Rub the stain into the foil. Coat tabletop with liquid plastic when thoroughly dry. Allow at least two hours of drying time before adding plastic. The plastic makes the table surface water-resistant.

Look how effective the gold foil collage is on the old oak table that was cut down to coffee table height. The window area behind table features a built-in seat that was collaged with orange and brown enamels. The result; the room takes on nice, golden hue. You can experiment with different color combinations using this technique. Try the idea on old wooden trays—given a collage treatment they become handsome gift items.

PICTURE FRAMES TO MAKE IN MINUTES

How many prints and photographs and pieces of children's art and pages from books do you have around your house—things you'd like to have hanging on your walls? Maybe you think framing them would be too much trouble or be too expensive. That's not true. Here are ten easy and beautiful ways you can "put them up."

Admittedly, some of these ideas take more minutes than others, but none requires much time, or much in the way of tools and skill, either. And the most expensive of them will cost only a couple of dollars in materials, so you can experiment to your heart's content. For complete instructions on each of these ideas, see page 167.

BAZAAR BEST SELLERS

These bazaar items fill the bill on every count. You can be sure that you will find something here for everyone in the family and gifts for friends, too.

1–2. Casserole carriers for toting a hot dish are sure sellers—easy to display. These are cleverly made in cotton.

3–6. Potholders make bright splashes for a kitchen. These are pretty enough to use under hot dishes at the dining table.

7. Imaginative hanging made of beads and lumber scraps adds color to a wall.

8. Kitchen gifts can be easy as well as useful. Spice rack, cut from cardboard, costs little to make.

9. Pencil caddy for desk at home or at office holds up to 20 pencils. Lift up; one glance tells you which ones need sharpening. Add gift tassels at the tops.

10. Egg cozy for three-minute eggs adds a bright look on the breakfast table. Cozy is made from felt scraps. You can use any color combination in felt that you wish.

11. Matchboxes—a smoker's delight. These are easily fashioned by gluing fabric to boxes. Colorful calicos, or any remn-

Much of the fun—and challenge—of a successful bazaar is in the selecting and the making of the items. Every one should be easy, appropriate as a gift, and big on eye appeal. And, every one should sell like hot cakes! Remember to include a lot of items that are small, require simple materials—this keeps the cost down. Color is an important factor, too. Don't be afraid to apply it lavishly—it'll help your bazaar sales.

ants can be used for matchboxes.

12–15. Placemats, unusual in their simplicity, make lovely backgrounds for pottery, china. To make placemats sell even faster, team them with matching napkins.

16. Christmas scroll working in rich colors of felt applique on burlap, re-creates the three Wise Men. The finishing trims are simple to add, yet furnish a dramatic look.

17–20. To make amusing and decorative door stops, simply take old bricks and give them a new look with covering of felt shaped in simple, smart designs.

21–22. Yardstick holder and phone book cover have colorful felt flower trims.

23–24. Hanging pincushions, whipped up from a wire whisk, can be made for a few cents, sold for at least a dollar.

25–29. Transform desk accessories into glamorous gifts by covering with fabric.

30–34. Smart ensemble is for a bedroom.

35–38. Toss pillows, trimmed with imagination, prove to be top-notch sellers.

39–40. Matching ruler and yardstick cases are simple to sew—anyone can do them.

See the following pages for additional information on how to make these items.

COMPLETE DIRECTIONS FOR BAZAAR BEST SELLERS

1-2. Casserole carriers. For round carrier: Cut a 17½-inch circle from quilted cotton. Finish edges with bias tape and rickrack. Space 8 curtain rings to edge, sew. Cut two pieces of bias tape 63 inches long; sew edges together. Thread both tapes through the rings. Sew ends of tapes together.

For oblong carrier: Cut 17½ by 17-inch rectangle. Fold right sides together to form a 17½ by 8½-inch rectangle. Stitch the short ends together by flat felling. Bind remaining opening with bias tape, rickrack. Stitch two 26-inch pieces of bias tape along edges. Fold in half; stitch to each folded corner. Tie ends to carry like basket.

3-6. Pot holders. Design pattern, trace front and back sections of fabric; cut. Cut two pieces flannel for double-layers padding. Cut front section applique. Trace and cut all applique motifs allowing 1 inch allowance on all sides. Stitch appliques.

Lay padding between wrong sides of top and bottom sections. Pin and baste around; machine stitch. Pin binding, baste, machine stitch one edge of bias tape to front of holder. Fold bias over edge to underside—hand-sew free edge to the back.

7. Painted wooden beads. Saw variety of wood shapes cut from dowels, sticks. Drill through with small bit. Buy wooden beads, too. Coat with undercoating, let dry. Paint with high gloss enamels. Use two or more colors on each piece. Thin paint, use tiny brush, add trim lines. When dry, string.

8. Spice rack. Cut triangle of cardboard 15 inches at base, 36 inches high. Cut two strips cardboard 2½ by 36 inches. Glue to sides of triangle. Cut 5 shelves each 2½ inches wide by 15, 11, 9, 7, and 5 inches long. Glue shelves to back and sides. Glue small strips balsa to fronts of shelves. Paint.

Cut rooster from shirt cardboard. Trim with calico, felt. Trim frame with rickrack. Glue rooster on top of the cabinet.

9. Pencil caddy. Cut 2 pieces perforated hardboard 8½ inches long by 3¼ inches wide. Keep holes equal distance from opposite sides when cutting. Enlarge all holes in top piece and corner holes only in bottom piece with 5/16-inch drill. Cut four 3-inch pieces of dowel. Insert in corner holes and glue. Paint. Trim pencils with tassels.

10. Egg cozy. Cut two bodies, wings from one color felt; cut comb, wattles, beaks of contrasting colors. Overcast bodies together from neck over back, sewing in beak, comb, and wattles. Attach wings with sequin trim. Sew sequin eye on each side of bird.

11. Matchboxes. You'll need cardboard box large enough to hold several small-size matchboxes. Measure sides of large box— starting at inside, adding ½ inch on all sides for overlap. Cut fabric pieces. Apply fabric glue to box. Ease fabric gently on outer side, smoothing carefully. Apply glue to inside of box, bend fabric over. Glue. Repeat with overlaps. Measure top of lid down back of box. Allow ½ inch for overlap on top, bottom, sides. Cut fabric, glue it. Cover lid tab, inside back, bottom, inside front, and front of box with another piece; paste overlap to underside of box. For top trim, cut rectangle of plywood, cover with burlap, glue on wood initials. For small matchboxes, cut one strip to cover from striking side across box and then around to striking place. Glue to box.

12. Burlap placemat. From 1 yard 36-inch burlap, cut mats to 15 by 18 inch size and fringe ½ inch all around. For white, black, orange stripes, mark lines on mat; paint with oil base paint. Use felt-tipped marking pen for thin black lines. For gold lines, glue on 2 layers ribbon, fringing ends.

13. Beige mats. Take 1½ yards 36-inch fabric; cut four 18x12-inch mats and four 14x14-inch napkins. Hem edges. Attach the orange and brown rickrack trim using three strands embroidery floss. With brown thread on each point of orange rickrack, take ¼ inch long stitch in center and two ¼ inch stitches on either side at angle. Make tiny stitch across end. Attach other rows of the rickrack using same crow's foot stitch.

14. Straw placemat. Cut 1 yard imitation straw fabric into four mats. Cut 10 strands pink and gold worsted, 1 yard long. Combine with equal length of 5 or 6 strands of gold cord. Knot about 4 inches below top of yarn. Braid strands until they're slightly longer than placemat. Knot again to hold yarn. Tie braids at top and bottom.

15. Fish mat. Cut 8 fish from 3 yards fabric. Mark trim lines on 4 pieces. Trim with small and large rickrack. Sew each of trimmed pieces to untrimmed piece with the right sides together, leaving 8 inches open at lower edge. Invert, hand-tack closed.

16. Hanging. Cut burlap to 40 by 20 inches. Cut 3 triangles of three colors felt 9 inches wide at base, $12\frac{1}{2}$ inches high. Glue on. Cut faces from three colors felt 3 inches at base, 5 inches high. Glue on. Glue on the lace, rickrack trims. Add crowns. Trim.

17-20. Doorstops. For sentry, eagle, and owl doorstops, select brick, measure, cover with felt. Do design pattern on paper, cut out felt designs in contrasting colors. Glue. For garden doorstop, glue piece of plastic foam to top. Cover top, bottom with felt. Cover sides with felt laced with two strips of matching color added in "basket weave." For flower stems, glue felt to florist wire. Add variety of felt flowers. Insert stems in plastic foam base.

21. Yardstick cover. Cut $37\frac{1}{4}$x$2\frac{1}{2}$-inch piece red, $36\frac{1}{4}$x2-inch piece white felt. Sew white piece over red. Add tab red felt and curtain ring. Add felt flowers, leaves.

22. Telephone book cover. Cut felt $\frac{1}{2}$ inch higher and 7 inches wider than phone book—use scalloping shears. Add ties for middle of book. Fold $3\frac{1}{2}$ inches in on each side and stitch "pockets." Slip book-size cardboards and covers into pockets. Add tree of felt flowers, flowerpot. Glue these on front.

23-24. Trim pincushions. Put wire whisk on right side of velvet. With eraser end of pencil, start at center and punch velvet up through whisk. Fill each puff as you go with cotton. Trim to $\frac{1}{2}$ inch of outer edge. Turn edges under and glue to bottom. Finish bottom with oval of velvet. Wrap the handles.

25-29. Remove ends from desk pad. Cover ends with flannel, then velvet allowing for 1-inch overlap. Cut flannel flowers, leaves. Cover long sides of pad with striped fabric. Replace ends. Add desk blotter.

Trim pen holder base with glued-on velvet. Apply flower motif. For note box, cover covers with flannel, then velvet. Cover the inside with two layers of printed cotton. Glue flower motif to lid of the box. Cover pencil box with striped fabric; add bias-strip trim, flower motif. Cover letter box with velvet, add striped bias strip.

30-34. Closet set. Boxes, wastebaskets vary so much in size that directions must be general. First, determine the amount of material you need, allowing for overlaps. The materials you use can be as varied as your imagination—wallpaper, silk, satin, cotton, denim, velvet, oilcloth. Wallpaper must be soaked on back with glue or wallpaper paste until it is flexible or it will tear. You'll need glue that can be thinned with water, braid, ribbon, and other trims.

35. Crewel pillow. Cut rectangle linen 18 x14 inches. Mark 11 guidelines. Embroider with chain stitch. Embroider three pairs of daisy stitches on alternating lines.

36. Spanish pillow. Cut triangle from each of four 10-inch felt squares. Stitch to make square. Add back of 12-inch square of any color used on front. Sew together, leaving 4-inch opening for filling. Fill. Tack the opening. Add tassels on the corners.

37. Zinnia pillow. Cut foam rubber to 12 inches in diameter. Cut 2 gold felt circles to 12 inches diameter. Mark off 2, 4, 6, and 8-inch circles on one gold felt piece.

Cut felt diamond shapes. For outside row, cut 16 $2\frac{1}{2}$-inch diamonds. For next row, cut 16 diamonds $2\frac{1}{2}$ inches outside and 2 inches inside. For next row, cut 16 diamonds $2\frac{1}{2}$ inches outside, $1\frac{1}{2}$ inches inside. For next row, cut 8 diamonds $2\frac{1}{2}$ inches both outside and inside. For center row, cut 8 diamonds $2\frac{1}{2}$ inches outside, $1\frac{1}{2}$ inches inside.

Fold diamond shapes tip to tip, leaving middle loose. Line two innermost bands with orange felt pieces (cut out inserts along folded edge of diamonds so lining will show). Stitch diamonds to circles on felt. Tack 3 dime-size green felt centers to "zinnia."

38. Anemone pillow. Cut 8-inch circle of foam. Cut two 8-inch circles of gold felt. Make one petal pattern on paper $4\frac{1}{2}$ inches long, one pattern slightly smaller about $4\frac{1}{4}$ inches long, a third one about 4 inches long. Using $4\frac{1}{2}$ inch pattern, cut 8 pieces of gold felt. Cut 8 orange petals $4\frac{1}{2}$ inches long. Cut 8 cotton batting 4 inches long. Insert cotton batting between orange and gold, sew together. Topstitch ends of petal to center of felt circle, overlapping petals. Cut center of gold, green circles, sew on.

39-40. Yardstick, ruler set. For the yardstick, cut canvas webbing 76 inches, decorative tape $37\frac{1}{2}$ inches. Sew. Trim. Ruler: webbing measures 27 inches long; decorative tape is 13 inches. Leave top of tape on both unsewed to hold the ruler and yardstick.

41. Golden owl, feathered with felt, is a wise choice for a carryall bag.

42–45. Small fry adore fun-to-play-with felt beanbags in familiar shapes. Octopus, gingerbread boy, horse, and cow are of felt.

46–47. Playful pillows do honors for toddler to teen-ager. Pockets on tic-tac-toe pillow hold the loose pieces, ready for play.

48–49. Stockings take their place on mantel or tree. Big ones trim outside door.

50–51. Knitted mittens with matching ear cover-ups are a hit as young gifts.

52–58. High school and college gals are partial to hug-me-tight dolls—especially the long, lanky, humorous ones.

59. Transform painted spools and wooden beads into playful little dolls.

60. Felt fish slippers are good travelers that fold flat. Hand-stitch pieces together. Cut them with a scalloping or with pinking shears; stitch on sequin trims.

61–62. Children love beanbags they can handle any way they like. Mr. and Mrs. Clown can be made of fabric remnants.

63. Retrieve Dad's worn shirts for artist's smocks. Cut off collar, sleeves, and shirttail. Hem; trim with storybook characters.

Gifts for the youngsters make up an important part of every bazaar. Stuffed toys, in clever animal shapes, please the very young and find favor among teen-age collectors too. Pillows for children's bedrooms, place marks for books, shoe carriers, and a host of other easy-to-fashion items are dependable sellers at bazaars. Check here for new ways to use color, new design ideas. Additional how-to is given on pages 100-101.

64. Terry topper for beach or bath is just the right size for four- to six-year-olds. Seam two kitchen terries at shoulders.

65–68. The Three Bears with Goldilocks by their side are a jolly foursome to sit on child's toy shelf. We dressed up oatmeal, ice cream cartons to hold little packages.

69–71. Don't overlook warm headgear for the winter sports. Choose bright colors.

72–74. Hat holders you can turn out by the gross are formed over balloons with crepe paper strips or paper towels, a quantity of liquid starch, some paper features, and much imagination. Bases are paper-covered weighted tin cans.

75. Piggy banks, to hold pennies, are simple gifts. Pig is made from a cardboard container with paper trim.

76–80. Place marks—boutique whimsies that are fashioned for bookworms.

81. Funny-face apron for playtime artists. It washes like a charm once you empty the pockets. Palm-tip strings tie at back.

82. Paint pail, covered with burlap, bright felt, holds a full-load of youngster's toy blocks. You can sew on letters, designs, or use a transparent white glue if you wish.

FOR BIG SPORTS

83-84. High-fashion cover-ups, either fabric or yarn, will be welcomed as a poncho.
85. This young lady's hat, fashioned from felt, can be worn or used as a center decoration to hold table tokens.
86. Beauty belt dresses up a simple frock. Yarn flowers are embroidered on burlap. Alter belt size with hook fasteners in back.
87-90. Garden or fireplace gloves. Finish fingers, cuffs of cotton work gloves with yarn. Trim with felt flowers or iron-on tape designs.
91. Booties are made from two terry finger towels. Ball fringe is only trim.
92. Turtleneck dickey is neatly ribbed at neckline and around bottom. Red yarn pompons add color and smartness.
93-97. There are endless ways for knitters and crocheters to contribute talents. Designs and colors in hats and purses must be varied to please variety of customers.
98-99. Hat and bag matchmates have great appeal to women. Cover inexpensive beach or garden hats and purses with fabric trims.
100. Watch your bazaar sales soar with inexpensive, easy-to-make masks, designed for hair-spraying time. Make of construc-

Show off the items for adults by grouping them together and displaying them with real flair. An attractive display will help sales. Make booths from leftover lumber and perforated hardboard. It's a good idea to leave plenty of space around booths so the shoppers can get close enough to see the small items. A coffee stand and a place to rest provide a welcome haven for shoppers and for the workers, the exhibitors, as well.

tion paper, cloth scraps, clear plastic wrap.
101–102. An impressive group of all-purpose tote bags is a must for a bazaar. Make some from canvas or duck, put the knitters to work, or make from drapery fabric.
103. Cover a hatbox with smart-looking fabric. Cover lid with harmonious oilcloth.
Line box and lid with paper; cover seams with passe-partout from your stationer.

104. Utility apron holds small tools in its generous-size pockets. Make soft stitched-on knee pads stuffed with several layers of quilt cotton.
105–106. Ivy League vests, patterned for parties, have no back—only a front. Sew on buttons that won't be used; trim. Make for teen-agers in school colors.
107. Carryall beach bag with one large

pocket and six small ones holds comb, hankie, candy bar, lotion, sunglasses; it's made of lightweight canvas. It wraps around waist with band tucked in.
108–109. Whimsical manikins cut from plywood on a portable jigsaw.
More information on items is given on the following pages.

99

BAZAAR BEST SELLERS

41. Carryall bag. Use as a purse, shoe bag, or for knitting. Make bag of felt from two rectangles olive green fabric. Cut felt flap of gold to fit across top width, scallop one edge. Cut matching scallops in assorted colors for feathers, two legs, one nose, two eyes. Assemble. Add handles.

42. Octopus beanbag. Cut two rounded bodies from felt, eight legs 6 to 9 inches long. Sew in legs as you stitch bottom of body—add felt "dots" with transparent glue.

43. Gingerbread boy. Draw shape 12 inches high—arms should extend 9½ inches. Cut two body shapes from brown felt. Trim front with rickrack, felt features, buttons. Assemble, adding beans. Fasten tie at top of head.

44-45. Horse, cow beanbags. Cut tails, legs, and horse's mane separately. Cut the bodies on the fold. Add eyes, cow's spots, before assembly. Sew legs, tails into bodies as you assemble. Add horse's mane last.

46-47. Playful pillows. Make tic-tac-toe pillow of red felt—use pinking shears to cut out squares. Cut design pieces of white felt, sew to pillow front. Make small pockets of red felt for pillow back—these hold the loose pieces. Stuff with cotton or foam.

Doll pillow features head that extends beyond pillow edge. Cut dress, hands, legs in one piece of red felt. Cut two circles for front and back of head and cotton batting for head's stuffing. Trim dress with a few rows white lace, buttons. Cut features for face and glue on. Sew dress, head to the front of felt square of pillow. Head should line up with outside edge. Hand-tack long felt strips for the doll's hair.

48-49. Stockings. Take orders for personalized ones at time of bazaar for later delivery. Names and surrounding patterns are cross-stitched on socks in coordinating colors. Or, cross-stitch "FILLUP" on stockings for time-of-the-bazaar sale. Add tassels.

52-58. Dolls. Red-riding-hood doll body, head are cut in one piece on the fold. Cut tops in arches; bottom is straight line, the hands, feet are cut separately as is hood:

Make a variety of humorous dolls for sale to teen-agers. Clothing, hair, features are added over basic body shapes. Make hair of yarn. Or, cut several different colors of felt circles, fasten centers, shred circles.

60. Felt fish slippers. Cut two soles and four fish-shaped sides. Use scalloping or pinking shears. Stitch on sequin trims before you assemble the slippers.

65-68. The Three Bears and Goldilocks. Bases are oatmeal boxes and ice cream cartons. They open to reveal tiny gifts. Cover cartons; stitch on long arms, legs. Glue on facial features. Stitch on hair, ears.

83. Poncho. From 1½ yards of medium-heavy cotton or wool, cut two pieces 27 by 15 inches. Sew short end of first piece to top of 27 inch end of second piece. Sew short end of second piece to long end of the first piece. Fold under raw edges. Turn hem, finish neck edge. Stitch 1 inch from the lower edge and then fringe around bottom.

KNITTING ABBREVIATIONS

k	knit
p	purl
st(s)	stitch(es)
sl	slip
in(s)	inch(es)
dec(s)	decrease(s)
inc(s)	increase(s)
beg	beginning
tog	together
psso	pass slipped stitch over
rnd	round
mc	main color
cc	contrasting color
dp	double-pointed needle

* repeat whatever follows the * as many times as specified.

84. Knit poncho. You'll need 6 ounces blue knitted worsted; 4 ounces each of turquoise, green, coral; 3 ounces each black, yellow; 1 pair No. 11 knitting needles. Gauge: 3½ sts = 1 inch; 5 rows = 1 inch. Blocking measurements: Each section measures 36 inches across lower edge, 6 inches across top. The length at center from lower edge to top of neckband is 17 inches.

Poncho section (make 4). Starting at lower edge with blue, cast on 126 sts. *1st and 2nd rows:* K across. *3rd row:* K 2 tog, k to last 2 sts, k 2 tog. *4th row:* P 2 tog, p to last 2 sts, p 2 tog. *5th and 6th rows:* Repeat 3rd and 4th rows. Break off blue. Leaving a 4-inch end for sewing, attach turquoise. *7th and 8th rows:* K with turquoise. Change to coral. *9th to 12th rows:* With coral repeat 3rd to 6th rows. Change to green. *13th to 18th rows:* With green repeat 1st to 6th rows. Change to turquoise. *19th and 20th rows:* K with turquoise.

Change to yellow. *21st and 22nd rows:* With yellow repeat 3rd and 4th rows. Change to black. *23rd and 24th rows:* With black repeat 3rd and 4th rows. Change to coral. *25th and 26th rows:* K with coral. Change to blue. *27th to 30th rows:* With blue repeat 3rd to 6th rows. Change to turquoise. Repeat 7th to 30th rows until 22 sts remain. K two rows with turquoise.

Neckband: Change to green. K one row, then work tightly in k 1, p 1, ribbing for 4 rows. Bind off tightly in ribbing.

Finishing: Block pieces to measurements. Sew the 4 sections together, matching the stripes. Press seams. Fringe: Cut 2 strands of one color each 9 inches long. Insert crochet hook through a cast-on st at lower edge and draw center of both the strands partway through to form loop. Bring ends through the loop and tighten. Using the 6 colors alternately, make fringe in every other st around the lower edge.

85. Dutch girl cap. Cut 11½x17¼ inch felt rectangle and fold 17¼ inch edge together to form triangle which will fold up for brim. Allow ⅝ inch seam allowance; glue edges of triangle together. Turn up brim at bottom, tack. Fold down point and glue. Trim with flowers, ribbons or invert it to hold small gifts to hang on the tree.

86. Embroidered belt. Take ¼ yard 36-inch-wide burlap, overcast edges to prevent raveling. Mark center of strip with long basting stitch. Embroider free-form flowers on strip same length as waist.

Centering embroidery, cut burlap 3 inches longer than waist measurement and 6½ inches wide. This allows 1 inch seam at each side and 1 inch overlap at back. Cut nonwoven interfacing 4½ inches wide and 2 inches shorter than length of burlap. Center interfacing on wrong side of burlap; baste in place.

Turn excess burlap to wrong side; press. Cut felt for underside same size as belt and sew. Overlap the ends 1 inch; to finish, add hooks, eyes.

91. Terry slippers. You'll need 1 each of red, white small terry towels. Draw boot-like pattern. Position on towel so points at center tops on all 4 sections are on a fringed corner. Seam allowance is 1 inch. Cut two sections from red, two from white.

For right foot, place red piece on top of white piece and straight stitch down the front, sole, and up back. Trim excess seam allowance. Turn and press. To make left foot, place white piece on top of red piece. Stitch and turn. Tack ball fringe to four top points.

92. Pompon dickey. You'll need 4 ounces white knitting worsted; 1 ounce scarlet; 1 pair of No. 8 needles; 1 set of No. 8 double-pointed needles. Gauge: 4 sts = 1 inch; 11 rows = 2 inches. Starting at lower edge of front with pair of needles, cast on 46 sts. Work 6 rows (3 ridges) of garter st (k each row). Then work as follows: *1st row:* K across. *2nd row:* K 3, p across to within last 3 sts, k 3. Repeat last 2 rows until total length is 5 inches, ending with 2nd row.

Next row: K across 38 sts. Slip last 30 sts knitted onto stitch holder for front; k remaining 8 sts for shoulder. Working over last set of sts only, continue as before for 1 inch, ending with p row. Break off. Attach yarn at opposite side of front neck and work other shoulder even for 1 inch, ending with a k row. On same needle cast on 30 sts for back of neck, work across 8 sts of other shoulder. There are 46 sts on needle. Work over these to match front. Bind off.

Turtleneck collar: With right side facing and first dp needle, pick up and k 30 sts along cast-on sts of back of neck, with 2nd dp needle pick up and k 8 sts along side of neck, k 30 sts from front holder, with 3rd needle pick up and knit 8 sts along other side of neck. Divide these 80 sts as follows: 28 sts on each of 1st and 2nd needles, 24 sts on 3rd needle. Mark beginning of rnd. Working in rnds, work in k 2, p 2 ribbing for 3 inches. *Next rnd:* * K 2, p 1, p and k in next st—a st increased. Repeat from * around. There are 100 sts. Work in pattern as follows: *1st rnd:* * K 2, p 3. Repeat from * around. Repeat this rnd until length of entire collar is 6 inches. Bind off loosely in ribbing.

Pompon (make 10): Wind scarlet yarn 25 times around two fingers, slip from fingers; tie strands securely around center. Cut the loops at each end and trim. Block. Sew a pompon to every other narrow rib.

CROCHETING ABBREVIATIONS: ch is chain; st is stitch; sc is single crochet; sl st is slip stitch; h dc is half double crochet; sp is space; dec is decrease; rnd is round; * repeat whatever follows the * as many times as specified.

BAZAAR BEST SELLERS

95. Knot stitch cap. You'll need 4 ounces knitting worsted, crochet hook size G. The gauge: 2 sps = 1 inch; 2 rows = 1 inch.

Base. Front piece: Starting at front edge, ch 64 to measure 16 inches. *1st row:* H dc in 6th ch from hook, * ch 1, skip next ch, h dc in next ch. Repeat from * across—30 sps— row measures 15½ inches. Ch 3, turn. *2nd row:* Skip first h dc, * h dc in next h dc, ch 1. Repeat from * across, ending with h dc in turning chain. Ch 3, turn. Repeat 2nd row until piece measures 5 inches. Break off and fasten.

Back: Turn work, attach yarn to 11th h dc from beginning of row, ch 3, work in pattern across center until 10 sps have been made. Ch 3, turn. Continue to work in pattern until there are 10 rows on back. Break off and fasten.

Work over base as follows: *1st row:* Attach yarn to bar of first h dc on first row of cap, sc in same place, * pull up a loop on hook to measure 1 inch, draw yarn through long loop, make an sc between long loop and single strand behind it—knot st made; sc around bar of next h dc. Repeat from * across, ending with sc under bar of last h dc or turning chain, as the case may be. *2nd row:* Make a knot st, sc under bar of first h dc on next row of base, make a knot st, sc under bar of next h dc, work knots sts and sc across as for first row. Continue in knot st pattern until each row is covered. With the wrong side facing, sew side edges of back to matching edges of front.

Border: With right side facing, attach yarn to base of first h dc at front corner, sc over bar of each h dc or turning chain around neck edge to opposite front corner. Ch 1, turn. *2nd and 3rd rows:* Sc in each sc across. Ch 1, turn. Now sl st in each sc across, then sl st in each ch across front of cap. Break off and fasten.

Cord (make 2): Make chain to measure 20 inches. Turn. Sl st in each ch across. Break off, fasten. Sew chain to each front corner.

96. Plaid beret. You'll need fingering yarn —3 ply—skein each black, gray, and white; 1 pair each No. 2 and No. 6 knitting needles; 10 bobbins. Gauge: On No. 6 needles, 6 sts = 1 inch; 8 rows = 1 inch.

Starting at lower edge with black and No. 2 needles, cast on 160 sts. Work in k 2, p 2 ribbing for 2½ inches. *Start plaid pattern:* Change to No. 6 needles. Wind 5 bobbins each with black and gray. *1st row:* Using bobbin for each color section, * k 16 black, k 16 gray. Repeat from * across. Hereafter when changing colors, always pick up next color from underneath dropped strand to avoid leaving a hole. *2nd row:* * P 16 gray, p 16 black. Repeat from * across. *3rd through 20th rows:* Repeat 1st and 2nd rows. *21st row:* Break off all strands. Wind 5 bobbins each with white and gray, * k 16 gray, k 16 white. Repeat from * across. *22nd row:* * P 16 white, p 16 gray. Repeat from * across. *23rd and 24th rows:* Repeat 21st and 22nd rows. *25th row:* Using colors as established, dec 1 st at center of each color section (10 sts decreased). *26th, 27th, and 28th rows:* Work even. *29th through 40th rows:* Repeat 25th through 28th rows 3 times more; 120 sts remain. Break off yarn. Wind white bobbins with black. Using black over gray sts and gray over white sts, dec 1 st at center of each color section on every k row until 20 sts remain on needle. Leaving an 18 inch length, break yarn and draw end through remaining sts. Pull up tight and fasten securely. Sew back seam with same colors. Press plaid pattern. Turn ribbing to wrong side.

97. Tassel hat. Materials: 4 ounces knitting worsted; No. 11 knitting needles; a double-pointed needle; small amounts of three contrasting yarns. Gauge: 3 sts = 1 inch; 5 rows = 1 inch. Directions: Cast on 88 sts. *Row 1:* (right side) p 2, * k 8, p 3; repeat from *, end k 8, p 1. *Row 2:* k 1, * p k, k 3; repeat from *, end p 8, k 2. *Row 3:* (first twist row) p 2, * slip next 4 sts to a dp needle, hold at front, k next 4 sts, k 4 sts from dp needle; p 3, repeat from *, end last repeat p 1. *Row 4:* same as row 2. *Row 5:* same as row 1. *Row 6:* same as row 2. Repeat these 6 rows for pattern until 8½ inches from beg., end with pat. row 1, having 4 rows above a twist row.

First dec row: (wrong side) k 1, * p 2 tog, p 2 tog, p 4, k 3; repeat from *, end last repeat k 2; 72 sts. *2nd twist row:* p 2, * slip next 3 sts to dp needle, hold at the front, k 3, k 3 from dp needle, p 3, repeat from *, end last repeat p 1. *Next row:* k 1, * p 6, k 3, repeat from *, end p 6, k 2.

Next row: p 2, * k 6, p 3, repeat from *, end k 6, p 1. *2nd dec row:* (wrong side) k 1, * p 2 tog, p 2 tog, p 2, k 2 tog, k 1, repeat from *, end last repeat k 2 tog, 48 sts.

3rd twist row: p 1, * slip next 2 sts to dp needle, hold at front, k 2, k 2 from dp needle, p 2, repeat from *, end last repeat p 1. *Next row:* k 1, * p 4, k 2, repeat from *, end p 4, k 1. *Next row:* p 1, * k 4, p 2, repeat from *, end k 4, p 1. *Next row:* K 1, * p 4, k 2, repeat from *, end p 4, k 1. Repeat 3rd twist row.

3rd dec row: (wrong side) k 1, * p 4, k 2 tog, repeat from *, end p 4, k 1, 41 sts. *4th dec row:* (right side) k 2 tog, * k 2 tog, k 1, repeat from * to end, 27 sts. Cut yarn, leaving 24 inch end.

Finishing: Run end through all sts and slip from needle. Draw up tight and run yarn through all sts again. Sew sides together. Block, stretching to 11 inches in width, 22 inches around, or desired headsize. Single crochet along outer edge. Form a ring of cardboard 2 inches wide and 4 inches in diameter. Place in top of cap, push top in and sew to hold below ring. With three contrasting colors, cut four pieces of yarn from each, 5 inches long. Braid colors and weave under cable st at base of ring. Make a tassel of each color and fasten to side of cap.

98–99. Burlap hat, bag. Start with inexpensive beach hat; cut burlap to cover hat using separate pieces for top of crown, side of crown and brim; glue down. Cut wide bias band from calico and fold under raw edge; glue around top of crown. Around bottom of crown, glue ball fringe and finish with a contrasting rickrack. Cut a strip of burlap from selvage edge to fit around the hat brim. Fringe opposite edge and glue down.

For flowers on hat, cut two circles from each of three different colors of calico about 3 inches in diameter. Cut three different lengths of wire from 4 to 7 inches. Cut two strips of green felt same length as each piece of wire. Glue 2 pieces of calico over cardboard and top of wire like a sandwich. Cover remainder of wire with felt; tack to brim of hat. Cut round felt circles; glue on to center of flowers. Cut leaves from a piece of green felt; glue to stems.

For tote bag: Draw basic bag pattern and cut 2 pieces each of burlap, calico, and non-woven interfacing from it. Place top of bag handle on fold. Cut piece of heavy cardboard and burlap from bottom pattern. Cut piece of calico about ¼ inch larger than bottom pattern to fold over sides and under cardboard.

Iron interfacing onto burlap to prevent raveling. Sew lining to burlap. Sew the side seams. Cut a straight strip of calico and sew a strip over seams on each side. Fold under raw edges. Cut a bias piece of burlap, bind top edges. Glue calico lining to heavy cardboard. Glue sides of burlap bag around underside of cardboard. Glue on burlap piece to finish bottom of bag. Glue ball fringe around bottom edge of bag, finish with rickrack. Cut 6 circles from calico. Vary sizes from 2½ to 3½ inches in diameter. Applique to bag. Cut felt circles for centers. Glue stems and leaves of felt to bag.

101. Vegetable tote bag. Cut two pieces canvas, duck, or sailcloth 14½ by 26 inches; sew together at short end. Sew on 8½ by 14½ inch piece of contrasting color, 3½ inches up from bottom seam. Fold under top and bottom edge. Draw simple-lined patterns of variety of vegetables. Cut applique designs and sew in place with vegetables on contrasting color, tops above. Sew side seams.

Turn inside out. Fold bottom of bag. Machine-stitch corners down with folds 3 inches from bottom seam. Fold down 2¼ inches of top for facing, and stitch (¼ inch seam allowance). Make 4 buttonholes in top double band (2 at sides, 2 in front and back). String 2 pieces 24 inch cord through holes; tie the ends to form loop.

107. Carryall beach bag. You'll need 1½ yards of canvas, matching thread, 3 contrasting colors of canvas 9 inches by 3¼ inches each (cut on selvage), iron-on tape.

From canvas, cut strip 5 inches wide by 1½ yards long and piece 11 inches by 26 inches (cut on selvage.) From each contrasting color, cut 9 by 3¼ inch strip.

Using iron-on mending tape, cut designs and apply to patches. Sew patches to large piece, making first one 1½ inches from top edge. Sew patches down at bottom and sides. Use zigzag stitch. Sew a line up center of each patch to make 2 small pockets.

Fold 11 x 26-inch piece with pockets to inside, allowing 1 inch extra length on back piece. Sew side seams. Turn; press.

Fold belt in half lengthwise, insert big pocket into belt fold; stitch down, turning under the raw edges.

CIRCUS TOYS

You can make a whole circus of animals and clowns to see at your bazaar. They're easy to produce and inexpensive, too. Early in the year, start saving boxes, cores from wax paper, aluminum foil, clear plastic wrap, plus remnants of fabrics. Then, when you're ready to start, you'll save a last-minute search for supplies. Glue and assorted papers and trims are about the only other supplies you will need. If you wish, make a tent for display.

Giraffe's body is formed with a toothpaste box. One continuous length of 12-inch core from wax-paper roll forms the front leg and neck. Toothpaste carton has holes cut in front through which core slips. Shorter core fits into hole, cutting into underside of body carton to form rear leg.

Cold-tablet box has circle cut out on underside through which the neck slips. Once assembled, elements are dismantled, covered with textured fabric, glued, reassembled. No. 3 paper fasteners, washers secure legs. Fasteners are inserted through both sides of body into hollow cores; heads of the fasteners are covered with black giraffe markings. Wire loops form ears and center horns. They're put between pieces of textured fabric, glued together, then glued in slits made in top of head. Nose and hoofs are black fabric—glued in place—as are body markings. Tail is made of unraveled cording.

"Happy" the clown has a paper-box body topped by a hat made of a typewriter ribbon container. Box is covered with black adhesive-backed paper. This paper is used for facial features, hair.

Paper ears are glued to sides of box. Short length of wire is inserted through typewriter ribbon box at center, folded several times inside, held with tape. Hat trim is cardboard circle between two pieces of adhesive paper; it was scalloped at edge to provide style. As a finishing touch, the small artificial daisy on wire end was added.

Fuzzy-faced lion's body is 3½ inches long—a cut-off salt box. A circular cardboard piece covers open end. Circular hole cut in box has wax-paper core inserted through body, extended about 1½ inches below to hold up body. Two 4⅝ inch core lengths form the legs, paws, and are crushed slightly to make oval shape. Once assembled, parts are dismantled, covered with textured fabric. Side legs are attached, even with body in back, to extending body core with No. 3 paper fasteners, washers. Fasteners are secured by working through core openings, then openings are covered with cardboard.

Ears are made the same way as the giraffe's. Face is circled with moss fringe glued in place to form mane. Whiskers are pipe cleaners.

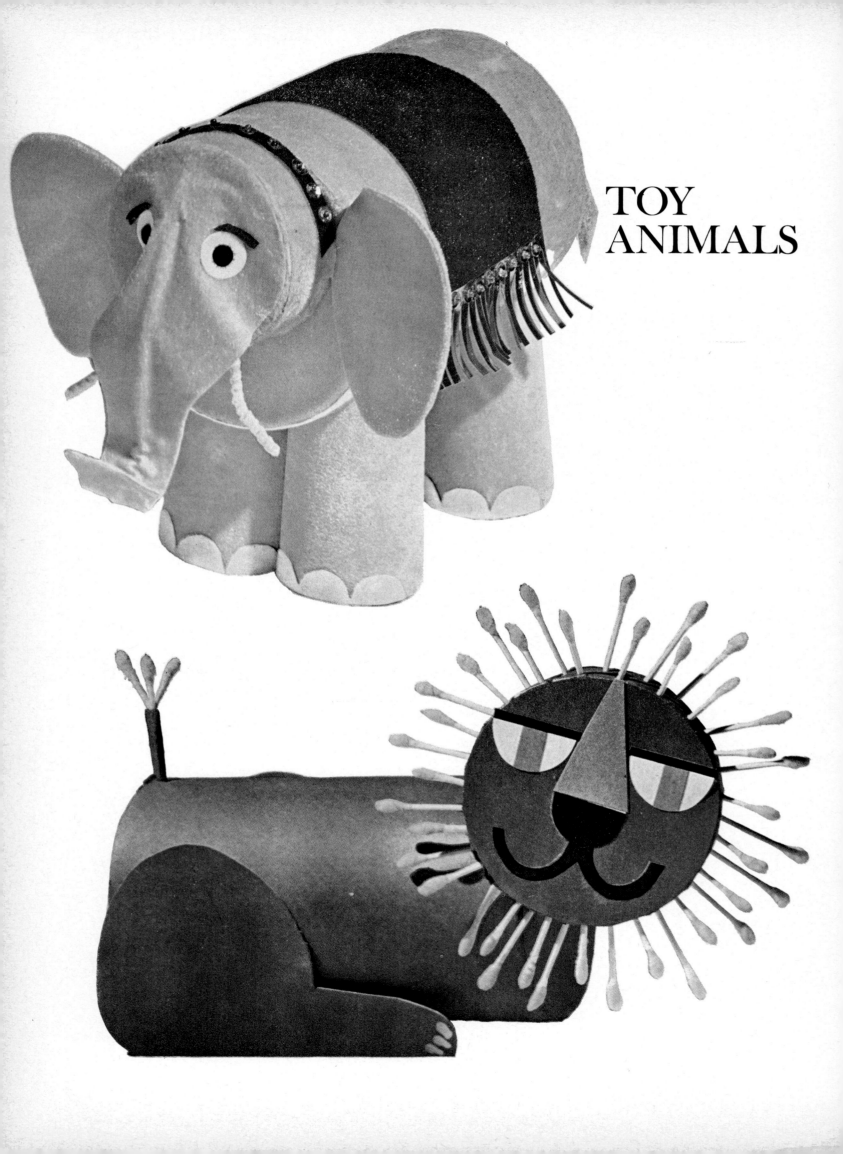

TOY
ANIMALS

Fanciful blue elephant has large powder, salt, or oatmeal container body. His legs are four 5½-inch-long cores of paper; his head is a typewriter ribbon container. Openings are cut into body to insert front, back legs. Core should be pushed all the way into body container, leaving 3¼-inch legs exposed outside. Depending on the box used for the body, front end is left open or is cut open for attachment of head, trunk, ready to be reglued later.

Pieces are dismantled to be covered with textured fabric. Two front, two back legs are inserted in body openings; joined together at seams; attached with No. 3 paper fasteners and washers. The work is done through hollow core openings. Bottom of typewriter ribbon box is attached to front cover of body with paper fasteners and washers. Front and sides of top section of container are covered with textured fabric for beginning of head. Remainder of head and the trunk is formed by cutting two pieces of fabric, shaped slightly larger than ribbon container at top, elongated into trunk at bottom. Pieces are glued together, sandwiching a piece of wire down the center from top of head to end of trunk. When dry, the top of head-trunk piece is glued around typewriter ribbon box top, letting material fold over the center wire so forehead protrudes outward. The ribbon container top is then slipped over the bottom section, glued. Designer: Ann Joselyn.

Red lion has a small-size oatmeal box body topped with a lid face. Head, body, and leg cut from shoe-box-weight cardboard are covered with colored paper. For body construction, the paper wraps around box with the ends extended over bottom rim. After the paper is glued to box, narrow strips are cut from the extending paper edge to box rim, folded over box rim, and glued.

Disk-shaped paper the same diameter as the box bottom is glued over the end to hide raw edges. Lion tail is paper rolled and glued, with cotton tip ends inserted in tip of tail. Face has paper strip glued around lid rim, edges overlapping. Strips are cut on both overlapped sides and glued to lid.

Colored paper disk is glued over the lid top to cover the strips, then face features are added. Mane is of cotton tips dipped in paint—these are inserted at various levels for a shaggy look.

Mock llama has a small-size oatmeal box body covered with colored paper. Legs, neck, and head made of shoe-box-weight cardboard are covered the same way, then are inserted into slits made with sharp knife. The tail is a twisted piece of colored paper.

Yellow spots, eyes, and blanket fringe are applied with poster-type paints. Use small brush for this detail work. Blanket is from construction paper.

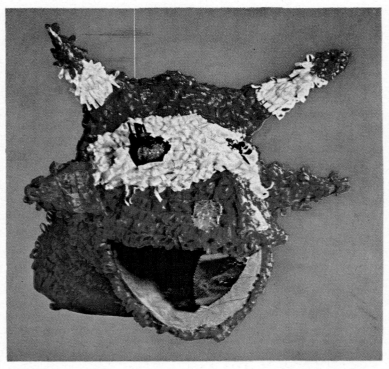

PINATAS

A traditional decoration from old Mexico makes a popular bazaar item. The decoration—the fun-filled pinata—will add to the color of your bazaar display; make a variety of shapes in rainbow colors.

Instead of hanging gifts from trees, Mexican people fill a gay pinata with presents, suspend it from tree limb, and let children take turns trying to hit it with a big stick until some lucky child contacts. At a pinata party, you can heighten the excitement by blindfolding player. The pinata may be raised, lowered to add to the fun.

In Mexico, breaking of the pinata climaxes each night of Los Posadas . . . a nine-day celebration before Christmas. Usually nine families join to celebrate the posadas with festivities occurring in a different home each night. Evenings begin when families meet to re-enact the Holy Family's search for lodging (posada). They form a procession, walk to a different house where they beg, by singing, to be asked inside. First they are refused, then finally are admitted to kneel before the Nacimiento or the Nativity scene to pray. Following the prayer, celebrating starts with dancing, food, and finally ends with pinata breaking.

When making your pinata, be sure that it is large enough to hold lots of little presents, durable to facilitate pulling up and down by a rope without falling apart, and fragile enough to shatter with two or three blows, and a good shape to decorate.

The true Mexican pinatas are formed around ollas (oh-yahs) or very thin, round clay pots. These are fired to shatter easily, thus they make ideal bases for pinatas. Unfortunately, the ollas are not available in most parts of the country. But, you can make your own olla, shape the design over it, and cover it with colorful paper.

Since ordinary clay flowerpots are usually too heavy and durable to make a pinata, the only way to use them is to tape two together as is illustrated in A below. To hang, lace string tied to a small stick through holes in the bases of the pots. With one firm blow, tape usually breaks, presents cascade down. The pots may shatter, too, so do not stand directly under them.

Cardboard boxes of shoe-box weight work well for pinata bases, too. You can cut a box apart, following drawings B or C below. Cut the box in half and tape it, or, you can cut out centers of sides, then cover with two thicknesses of newspaper. The "trap-door" technique shown in drawing D is another way to handle the box.

Large paper bags convert easily to pinatas. However, they aren't completely satisfactory for energetic stick wielders as they are more likely to rip than break. A paper bag works well for triangular shapes as E illustrates. Cover by folding tissue or crepe paper in half, fringing. Attach the fringed pieces to bag base. This technique is faster than some of the others—try it for birthday-party favors.

For making cone shapes like ears of bull above, roll newspaper cones, as in F.

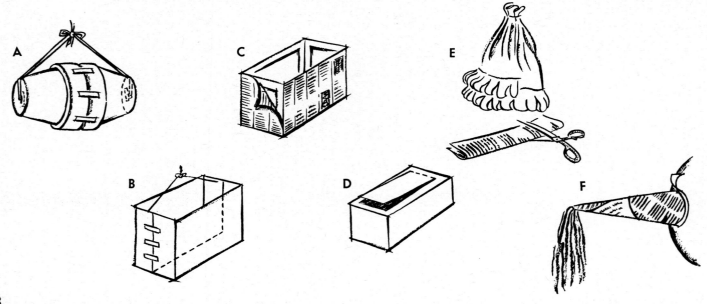

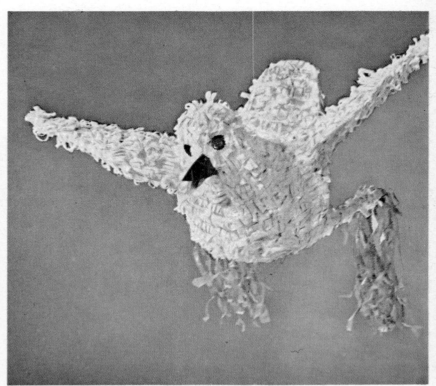

White dove, symbolic of peace, will soar over festivities at a pinata party; also will be brisk seller at the bazaar. It's good for the holidays.

Cheery pink elephant like this one will capture attention at a holiday bazaar. Make one for yourself, too, and use it as theme-setter at a party.

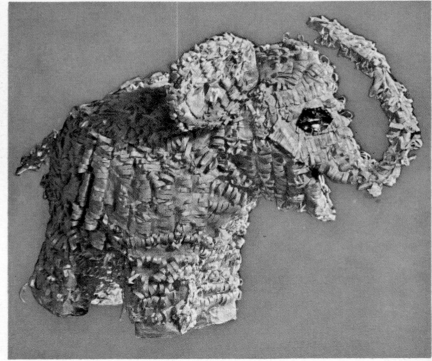

Bright-colored clown is a typical Mexican pinata—favorite of children. The bull, opposite page, would thrill any child, too, with its vivid colors.

Friendly lion picture will delight both boys and girls. Designed by Sue Hodgdon, lion is stitched to cotton ticking background that has been tightly stretched on a wood frame. Design was first sketched on paper, then transferred to the ticking with red pencil.

Inexpensive rug wool yarn loops create mane, tail, and a beard. Long running stitches form body of lion. Lightweight black wool outlines the figure. Lightweight wool chain stitches produce delightful butterfly.

Walnut-stained toy chest was designed by Ward Mayborn using leftover wood. To copy, cut 6 plywood rectangles . . . two 26″x22″ pieces for front and back . . . two 20″x22″ pieces for the sides, and two 20″x26″ pieces for top and bottom. Sand edges smoothly and nail together fitting edges and corners neatly. Apply hinges so lid may open a full 270 degrees.

Glue on 1″ deep wood blocks and 1″ wide by 2″ deep strips of wood, then secure with tiny nails. Use wood initial to personalize chest. Countersink all nails for more attractive look. Stain chest with dark walnut.

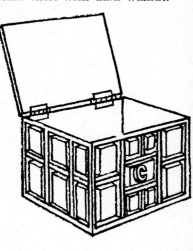

Happy wall hangings make good gifts for children. For the very small, animal and circus figures are especially welcome. A less permanent wall hanging can show whimsical humor such as the straw funny face on the opposite page. This can be used at Christmastime for a holiday trim—or, it would go in a playroom the year-round.

GIFTS FOR CHILDREN

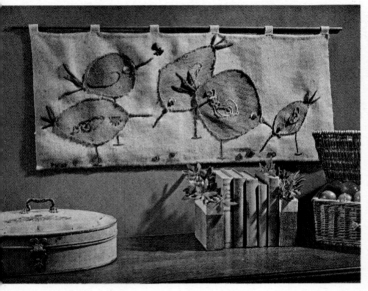

Stylized sandpipers playfully peck away on this burlap wall hanging designed by Peggy Waters for her son's bedroom.

Background of burlap measures 17½"x39". Panel hangs from a wood dowel laced through six burlap loops made by folding fabric to 1" wide bands measuring 3" long from end to end.

Birds are first cut out of burlap, then appliqued to backing with yarn. Beaks, legs, and butterfly are chain-stitched. The largest bird measures 10"x6½"; next bird is 9½"x9½"; others are 6"x3½"; 9"x6"; 7"x5½". Muslin lines loops, backs the panel.

Purple feline looks as if he's "the cat that just ate the sardines." And maybe he did . . . notice the fish.

To copy this tapestry created by Mrs. Jane A. Perego, stretch textured linen or burlap fabric over frame of wood. Outline cat's body, tail, head, and ears with looped stitch. Repeat looping on small areas within cat.

Fill in other areas with running stitches, satin stitches, and French knots. Invert hooking needle on the cheeks, around eyes, and inside body areas for smooth, solid effect. Applique small patches of felt for fish, ears, nose, squares inside body.

Imaginative face will delight and amuse your children, the children of friends. Once you've copied this gay face, you'll want to make several of them, combining shapes, textures, and colors to suit your fancy.

Designer Robert Winquist of Manhattan Beach, California, originated this "creature of fantasy" using ordinary materials found around home. The background is a round, plastic-straw placemat. Or, you can use natural straw fan if you wish. The rest of the materials include coasters for eyes, ribbon for top of head, a plastic-foam ball for nose, an oval placemat for tongue, and glue.

Adhere the plastic placemat tongue in place to straw background using a household glue. Black paper dot pupils glue to the coaster eyes. White foam nose and finished eyes glue to background, as does hair ribbon. The face hangs with hook-wire assembly.

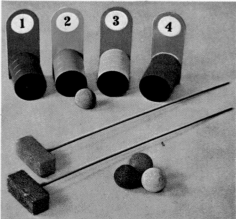

Simple pool game is cut from hardboard (or plywood) with tin cans placed in opening in the four corners. Plastic foam balls are used with wooden dowel cue sticks. Use on a card table or floor. **Living room golf game** is made from one-pound coffee cans. Glue cardboard piece at end of can, add number cut from calendar. Plastic-foam balls are hit with dowel-plastic-foam mallets.

THESE ARE SPECIAL GAMES; THEY ARE QUICK TO MAKE

You can make special games for Christmas gifts, birthday presents, or family room fun. All of these are simple to create, are sure to please.

Turn your talents to fashioning a complete puppet show, or try a television stage and marionettes. Ring-toss is a popular pastime for the younger members of the family; while the golf and pool will appeal to older boys.

Team puppets and a candy-sprinkled stage. A sturdy cardboard box is painted with pink enamel, decorated with icing, hard candy.

The players range from a reindeer with sweet tooth to candy sprites. Puppets are cut from felt; reinforced with pop sticks glued at back.

Puppets and marionettes, elfin and easy to make, call for 8-inch plastic foam balls as the main ingredient. To make: cut balls in half and line interior with felt for hinge.

Attach strings at the top and bottom for marionettes.

For puppets, cut a grip for four fingers in top, a hole for thumb at bottom. Trim with burlap and buttons. Television stage is made from a velvet-lined box.

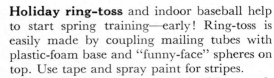

Holiday ring-toss and indoor baseball help to start spring training—early! Ring-toss is easily made by coupling mailing tubes with plastic-foam base and "funny-face" spheres on top. Use tape and spray paint for stripes.

Baseball game is constructed with a cardboard box of any size. Cut holes large enough to admit plastic balls and assign numbers.

For the returning device, cut 6 or 8 inches from the front panel, then glue a piece of cardboard at an angle on the inside. Use against a wall in basement, play room, or family room.

HERE ARE SOME PROJECTS DAD MIGHT NOT THINK HE CAN DO— BUT HE CAN

Dad's workshop can yield small and large wonders for gifts. Try the inexpensive trim-a-trunk project for a start: Or, make accessories for the sewing room. A basket table to hold wool or fabric and a wicker basket thread holder for wall are good team. Line hanging basket with felt and pierce with knitting needles which dispense spools of all sizes, also hold the rickrack and trims that are used in sewing.

The portable playhouse provides hours of fun for tots. It disassembles easily for no-fuss storage.

The playhouse, opposite page, is made from six 48-inch pieces of marine plywood. (Three 4- by 8-foot sheets are cut in half.) Each of the square panels has two ½-inch slots cut four inches in from each side halfway down each panel. Each panel interlocks with the next at right angles. For entry, a 30-inch diameter hole is cut in the front and back panels.

A roof piece made from a 1-inch by 4-inch piece joined to a 1-by-2-inch piece is placed at point where the two roof panels meet. Simple designs can be applied to the panels with stencil, paint.

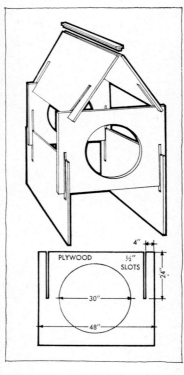

Metal foot lockers are emblazoned with different designs to suit each child.

Use bright flowers for a girl, a military look for a boy. Work with stencils and metallic spray paint. Let paint dry at each stage.

Sewing table. Have lumber dealer cut two 24-inch circles from plywood. From center of these, cut 20-inch circles. You'll have two 24-inch circles 4 inches wide. Glue pieces together; clamp and let dry overnight.

Screw legs in place. Use either three or four. Paint table in bright color. Glue a 2-inch piece of plastic on outside circumference of table. Cut strips of felt to put between reeds of basket. Place basket in hole of circle.

Checkerboard is colorful as well as handy to have at game time.

The checkerboard is made from painted plywood. Tissue squares in contrasting colors are applied with clear plastic spray or varnish.

Any color combination you wish can work effectively. This red and yellow scheme is a gay choice. Or, use a traditional, red, black color combination.

The checkers are easy to make. They are of one-inch dowels which are sanded smooth. Art paper is glued on tops. Varnish is added last.

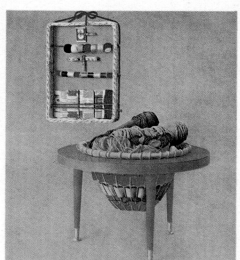

Three handsome pedestal stands are salvaged from old oak newel posts. To adapt this idea, cut the posts to the height you desire and glue and nail on the square top platforms. Trim with wooden knobs at each corner. Sand and repaint in brilliant hues. Or, stain if the wood grain is interesting.

Amiable animals—a tiger and an elephant—make delightful benches for a tot's room.

To duplicate these animals, have the lumber dealer cut oblongs for bodies and round or square heads. Cut out rectangles to shape the four legs. Nail the five sides of the body together and nail on the head. Sand all edges until they are smooth.

Paint the animal a bright color. Then, using a small brush for detailed work, paint on eyes, ears, other finishing touches. Or, you can use bright designs cut from felt and glue them on. Ball fringe is effective trim, too.

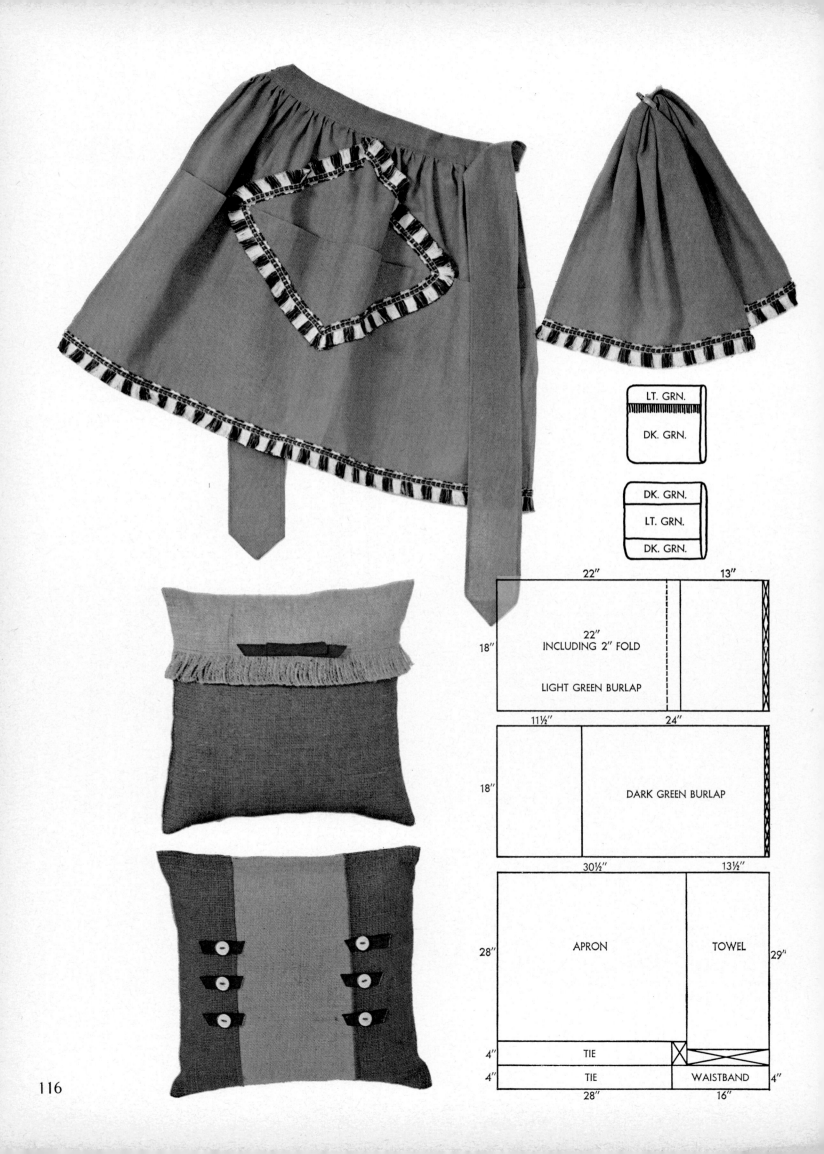

LT. GRN.

DK. GRN.

DK. GRN.

LT. GRN.

DK. GRN.

22″   13″

18″   22″
INCLUDING 2″ FOLD

LIGHT GREEN BURLAP

11½″   24″

18″   DARK GREEN BURLAP

30½″   13½″

28″   APRON   TOWEL   29″

4″   TIE

4″   TIE   WAISTBAND   4″

28″   16″

GIFT IDEAS
FOR WOMEN

Six placemats from a yard. To copy attractive-but-easy-to-do idea, cut 1 yard of 36" wide, linen-like fabric into six rectangles measuring 12"x18", using entire yard of fabric. Make running stitch with sewing machine (or by hand) around each rectangle, spaced about ¾" in from all edges. Fringe edges to stitching.

Cut floral designs from decorator fabrics in brilliant colors that complement placemats. Be sure to leave a small border around each flower or flower cluster. Fold under this extra border, then place design on corner of a placemat. Slip-stitch around edge to secure.

Apron with matching towel from a yard. To make this handsome pair, cut a 30½"x28" long rectangle from 44" wide yard of rough textured fabric. (See pattern, opposite.) Make narrow hems at sides and bottom. Fold up the length of the fabric 5" to form a long pocket 7" from the top of the apron, extending the width of the apron. Topstitch the fold in place at each side.

Topstitch the multicolored fringe trim to the apron in a diamond shape in the center area for decoration and to form the three pockets. Topstitch the multicolored fringe trim to the bottom of the apron, too. Gather the top of the apron to a 16"x4" waistband. Fold over the waistband and stitch in place, catching in the previously hemmed ties. Apron ties should be cut 4" wide by 28".

String finished towel through the loop of a brass cafe-curtain ring which can clip to the waistband of the apron. In this way the towel is always handy for use, yet can be easily removed from the ring for laundering.

Pair of toss pillows from a yard. To reproduce this ingenious pair, color coordinate them so that they can be used together or across the room from each other.

For fringed toss pillow, cut 18"x22" rectangle from ½ yard light green burlap. (See pattern.) Fold over 2" on 22" measurement. Cut darker green burlap piece 18"x 11½". Overlap 2" fold of light green burlap on darker green burlap. Stitch burlap pieces together 1¾" in from edge of fold. Fold entire length of the fabric in half keeping right side together.

Sew the three open sides closed, leaving an opening in one side for insertion of the pillow. Cut horizontal threads in the 2" overlapped fold of light green burlap and draw out the horizontal threads to form folded fringe trim. Make a bow of velvet ribbon and tack it in place in the center of the fringed area.

For reproducing the buttoned toss pillow, cut an 18" x13" piece from remainder of the light green burlap. Fold the darker green burlap over the light green burlap, then top-stitch in place making tubular form. Center the light green burlap within pillow top area. Sew two sides closed, leaving enough of an opening for insertion of pillow. Sew three buttons to each side of center stripe. Take 2¼" lengths of velvet ribbon and make a slit in the center of the ribbon the same diameter as the button. Slip ribbon over the button for a bow effect. Insert the pillow form in the opening and sew the opening closed.

Designer of gifts was Ann Joselyn.

TOTE BAGS FOR HOME AND BEACH

Black and brown bag with fringed ends is easily made by folding in half one each 36 inch by 12 inch pieces of black and brown burlap and seaming sides; folding down and fringing edges; adding the handles.

Striped tote bag is roomy enough to hold needed yarn for a bulky knit sweater or your swimming doodads. Smooth inside lining and base allow yarn to unwind freely for the knitter, are waterproof for the swimmer. Might as well make up several while your machine is open! You can get eight linings from 72″x72″ shower curtain.

To reproduce bag, cover base by centering cardboard 2 between two pieces of plastic 1, right sides out. Pin in place around edge, stretching tightly. Lay base on tissue paper for sewing (plastic clings and cannot feed through machine). Attach zipper foot, stitch as close as possible around cardboard edges. Tear off tissue paper.

Next, stitch short sides of lining piece 3 together. Stitch outer fabric 3, right sides together. Press seam and turn right side out. Lay flat with seam at one side. Using yardstick, place chalk marks on lower edge of fabric 6¼″ and 14¼″ from seam. Strap ends will be attached here. Measure down 4¼″ from top edge, mark 6¼″ and 14¼″ from seam. Loops will be centered here.

Now, center oilcloth 5 down length of wrong side of fabric strip 4. Fold and press fabric over edge of oilcloth down full length. Turn under raw edges of fabric until about ¼″ remains along side edge. Pin in place, always being careful not to pierce oilcloth, and machine-stitch close to center edge. Repeat down other side.

Then, fold in one-third width of material loop 6 entire length of strip. Press. Fold other edge at line where first edge reached. Press again. Double under about half of last third; stitch along edge. (Stitching will be down center of loop.) Cut strip into four equal lengths. With each, double ends under so loop measures 1½″ when flattened. Hand-stitch several stitches to hold. Center loops or chalk marks at upper edge of bag; hand-stitch both ends of underneath side of loops to the bag. Thread the straps through.

Next, with wrong side out, pin *right* edge of lining to seam allowance of base. (Center side seam at middle of base end.) Turn base over. With wrong side of fabric out, pin *right* lower edge to that side of base. Base seam allowances are now between *right* side edges of lining and

Finish bag by turning outer fabric right side out and stretching up along with straps until both are smooth and taut from base up. Hand-stitch straps to bag fabric through center back of loop. Stretch up lining and outer fabric together in same way; pin near top on fabric side. Fold fabric over top of lining. Turn under raw edge of fabric 1″, pin on inside. Remove outside pins. Machine-stitch close to edge on inside. Press top edge of bag. The designer was Elizabeth Noah.

fabric. Slip four strap ends through at chalk marks. Pin in place between fabric and base. Attach zipper foot and stitch through all layers as close to cardboard as possible.

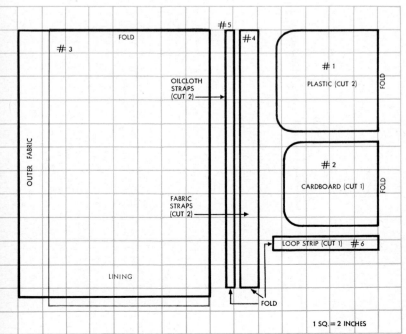

Felt orchid and poinsettia flowers on natural burlap panels are two more alternates for the flower-bedecked tote bag shown on the opposite page. Designed by Ann Joselyn, the panels may be made with snaps to make them interchangeable as seasons, costumes change.

To copy the pink lined bag shown opposite, cut burlap and lining pieces 22½″x15½″. Fold burlap over; stitch 15½″ angles together to form tube. Stitch bottom edges together; press seams flat. Flatten bottom section with bottom seam centered, then stitch a 3″ seam at each corner. Trim off triangle extensions above seam. Turn the bag inside out. Make lining same way.

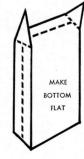

Place 3″x6½″ cardboard in bottom of bag for support. Cut burlap piece 6½″x 12″ to form the pocket. Stitch around the piece ½″ from the edge. Fringe the edges. Sew to front of bag leaving top open to form pocket. Insert the lining; topstitch to burlap bag at top edges; catch 1½″x 13″ lined straps at either side.

For interchangeable side panels, use snaps to attach panels to bag sides. The flowers are cut from felt, following simple pattern. Do pattern freehand on paper first. Glue the flowers to burlap.

Machine-stitched trims can be applied in a hurry. A collection of mats in various color combinations is nice to have for your linen trousseau. Keep the color and design of your tableware and accessories in mind when you plan the mats. Close attention to color and design details will result in a beautifully appointed table.

This blue-and-violet combination on machine-stitched mat would be ideal for a lilac luncheon in the spring—make matching blue napkins to complete the set.

Pep up your table with a wardrobe of made-by-you placemats. One of the easiest ways to give table settings a new look is to vary the color, shape, or design of the placemats. These simple-to-copy ideas will help you start.

IDEAS FOR A VARIETY OF PLACEMATS

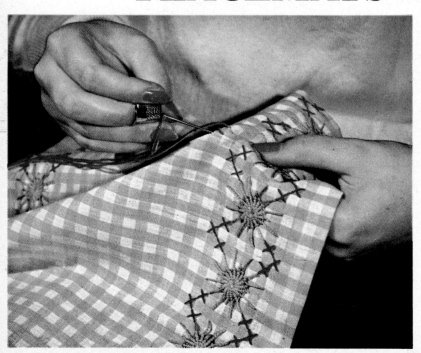

Spray-painted mats are unusual; you get outstanding design effects with little effort. The first step is to cut the stencils—be sure to test the design on mat-sized paper first to check the finished appearance. Then, spray the mats, letting each color dry before proceeding.

Cross-stitch on gingham works up fast. See how effective the green and red design is on yellow-checked fabric. Use any favorite embroidery pattern for the design.

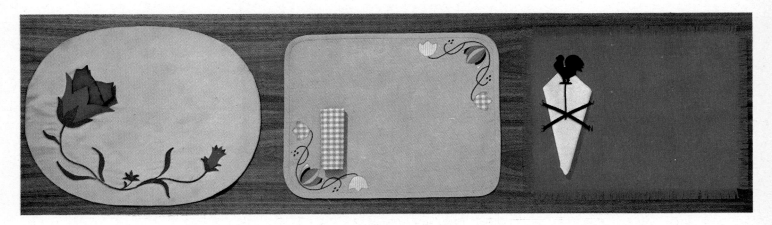

Fresh-as-spring tulip design, blooming with machine-stitching, pockets a napkin. For variety, make flowers in contrasting shades. After you master this technique, try the graceful swirls on pillows, a full-size tablecloth for dinners, a table runner, or use it to border a set of kitchen curtains. Color-key the curtains to the room's decorating scheme.

Pretty-as-a-posy mat, center above, is charming with its simple detail and crisp appearance. It makes an interesting setting for any season. Use on a bare table or on a solid-colored tablecloth. Make matching napkins.

You'll crow with delight at the clever mats, right above, that add a cheery note to breakfasts. A weathervane of black felt holds napkin in place. Reinforce the weathervane with florists' wire. Edges of the placemat are fringed to a ¾ inch depth all around. Napkin has machine-rolled hems. Color scheme is dramatic.

There's no needlework on the three mats shown directly below. Design at far left is on felt, is done in a hurry. Felt's ravel-resistant edge needs no hemming. Cut a stencil from stiff paper then anchor with pins or with double-faced tape. Glue felt leaves to bamboo motif.

The most familiar designs are often the smartest. The apples, above center, rest on a white mat. The design often will dictate the color to use. These rosy-red apples have a fine mist of yellow sprayed on. Green and black outline the stems and leaves. Use red or green napkin.

Quail posing on placemat, above right, will appeal to masculine tastes. Gleaming rhinestone eye is glued into the design. It's a good idea to protect your table with a stack of newspapers before spraying stencil with fabric paint. The papers will catch any fallout spray.

Only the simplest kind of hand-stitching is needed to apply the smart designs shown on the three mats below.

Bias-tape blossoms, left below, are used on a beautiful shade of blue to add springtime beauty to a table. The flowers are daintily hand-stitched in place. For tricolored napkin, sew three sections of fabric together.

For barbecues or breakfasts, use a striped denim ticking with a ball-fringe border. Mat and napkin are machine-hemmed; the ball-fringe trim is sewed on by hand.

Balloon motif, a natural for a party table, is made from yarn. For "balloons," wind a piece of yarn into a flat circle until desired diameter is achieved. Leave area for "string" to extend down from balloon. Overcast yarn balloons, strings to mat. Designer: Ann Joselyn.

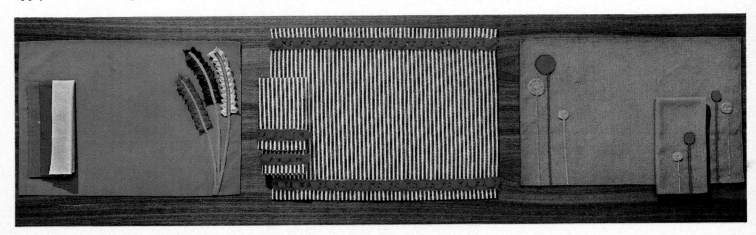

PLACEMATS TO USE EVERYDAY

Mats make attractive gifts that may be used for breakfasts, luncheons, or casual suppers. One place setting of holly leaf mat, below, requires ½ yard tarlatan and white, green, and red thread. To make, draw thread to square fabric pieces. Cut the green linen piece 17″ x 16″, two white linen pieces 5″x16″, six green linen pieces 3″x3″, and ten red linen pieces 2″x2″. For guideline, draw thread 1″ in from four sides green, white linen pieces. Place two 5″x16″ pieces on opposite ends of the green piece, aligning 16″ edges and matching the drawn threads.

Baste in place. Cut tarlatan piece; place under the mat. Applique around the green linen in a zigzag stitch, and stitch along drawn thread line; trim 1″ margin of white linen underneath, 1″ margin of green linen on top side of mat. Applique around the white linen edges, following drawn thread line. Trim the extra

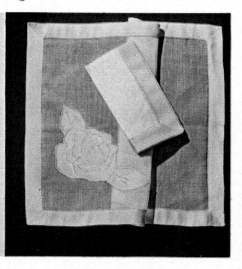

fabric on four sides of mat, close to stitching. For holly leaf, place pattern onto green 3″x3″ linen square; machine-pierce the design; remove paper pattern. Center; baste design pieces onto white linen borders. Applique around design; trim extra fabric on four sides of mat, close to stitching. Follow same procedure for red berries. Arrange, baste pierced berry patterns around holly leaves. Applique; trim extra material. Finally, cut away tarlatan from back of the mat.

Rose applique placemat setting, above, requires ½ yard white organdy, ¼ yard pink polished cotton. To make, cut the organdy 14″x18″, and 6″ square of pink polished cotton. Trace the rose design (copied from garden catalog) and put pattern on cotton. Applique around the outside edge of rose in the placemat corner. Position 2″ in from side and lower edge, using hand stitch or machine decorator set for narrow zigzag stitch. Using a white cotton thread, straight stitch inside lines from reverse side of pattern. Pull threads to the wrong side. Now cut pink cotton facing 1½″ wide, stitch to wrong side edge. Miter corner, turn to right side, turn under the edge ¼″, stitching flat. Finally, cut napkins of organdy 12″x12″; apply facing of pink polished cotton the same way you applied facing on the placemat.

For four blue-white settings, you'll need 1½ yards white linen, 2 yards each blue linen, stiff lining, contrasting thread. Cut 18″x14″ mats; lining same. Baste organdy under area to be decorated; stitch decoratively. Stitch to lining leaving side open to slip-stitch. Cut 13″x13″ napkins and decorate.

Four orange settings, above, need ⅔ yard rough-weave material, ⅞ yard white linen, 9 yards braid. Cut 18″x12″ mats, 14″x14″ napkins. Stitch ¼″ hem in right side of mats; topstitch braid. Add braid to napkins.
Gold placemats, right bottom, take 1½ yards gold linen, 14 yards rickrack for four settings. Cut 18″x12″ mats and 14″x14″ napkins. Stitch through center rickrack on right side. Fold, press to wrong side. Top stitch to finish.

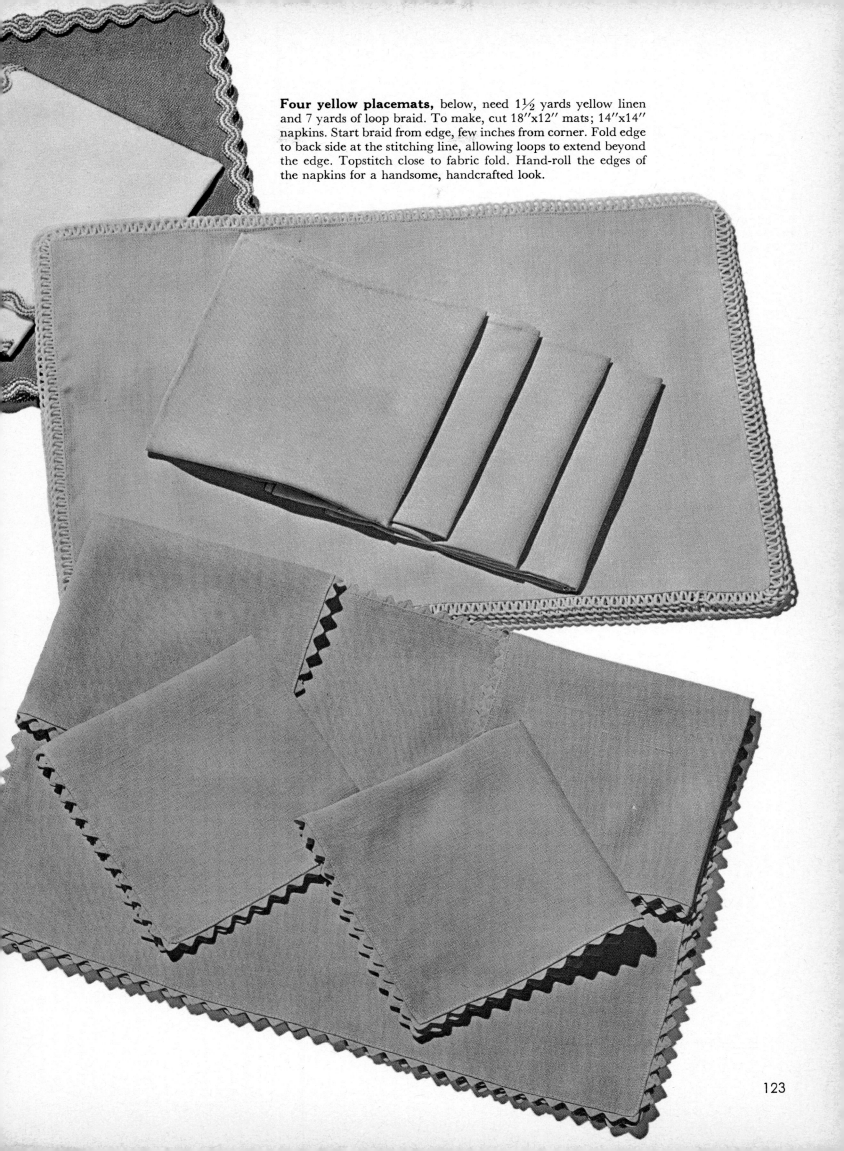

Four yellow placemats, below, need 1½ yards yellow linen and 7 yards of loop braid. To make, cut 18″x12″ mats; 14″x14″ napkins. Start braid from edge, few inches from corner. Fold edge to back side at the stitching line, allowing loops to extend beyond the edge. Topstitch close to fabric fold. Hand-roll the edges of the napkins for a handsome, handcrafted look.

For people who love to cook and love to give parties, a dinner table, luncheon, or a barbecue should always be a triumph. The clever homemaker knows that any food looks and tastes better when it's served in a charming setting. Colorful and inexpensive placemats and napkins can add immeasurably to the attractive appearance.

One simple hint on settings: Don't try to match floral patterns on china or pottery with heavily-patterned placemats and masses of matching flowers in a flower arrangement on the table.

ATTRACTIVE PLACEMATS

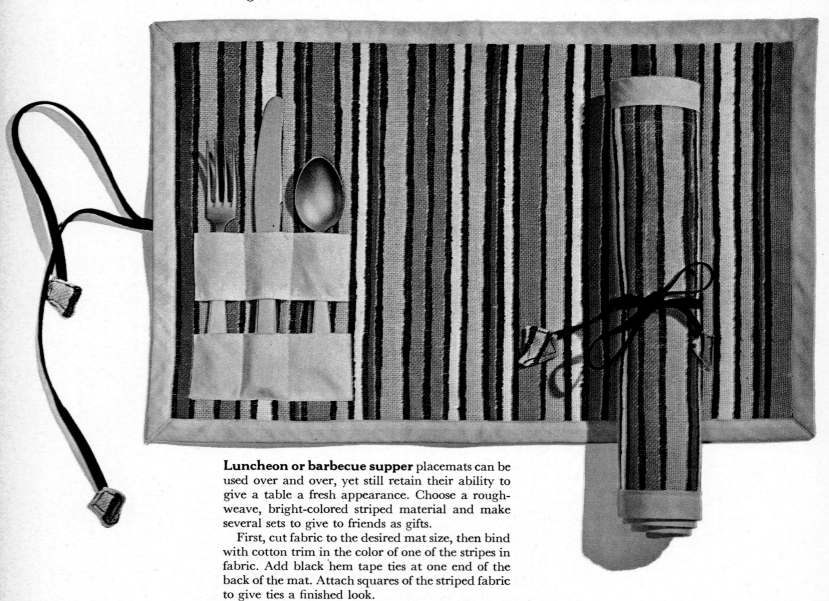

Luncheon or barbecue supper placemats can be used over and over, yet still retain their ability to give a table a fresh appearance. Choose a rough-weave, bright-colored striped material and make several sets to give to friends as gifts.

First, cut fabric to the desired mat size, then bind with cotton trim in the color of one of the stripes in fabric. Add black hem tape ties at one end of the back of the mat. Attach squares of the striped fabric to give ties a finished look.

Stitch on two strips of the same color fabric you used to bind mats to make holder for the flatware. Make "pockets" for knife, fork, and spoon. For barbecues or buffet dinners, the mats containing silverware are rolled, tied for guests to pick up along with a plate of food. Napkins of the bold striped fabric would be nice addition to the set. The designer of placemat: Ann Joselyn.

For a coordinated color scheme at a special dinner, use not-so-common color combinations in mats and napkins. Try this color mixture of blue mats that are decorated with purple and green tape trim. Arrange the tape into shapes of stylized stars. One band of tape will effectively trim the matching napkin. For added color accent, form purple and green ribbon flowers to serve at bottom of candles on table.

Another way to trim mats and napkins is to team a set of rickrack stars and abstract designs made of white tape. Start with medium green mats and napkins and use a white-and-gold combination of trims.

Rough-weave fabric placemats with contrasting color inserts feature designs that symbolize the four seasons. The designs by Ann Joselyn are embroidered with related colors of thread. Make your mats any size you wish, then machine- or hand-embroider the designs. For spring, try two tulips done in orange and black. Summer is indicated by a set of seashells in black and white. Fall shows interlocked wheat stalks, while the winter is symbolized by handsome snowflakes.

Ideal to wear for smorgasbord party

GREECE

GOTLAND · SWEDEN

Greek or not, she'll love wearing it!

Scandinavian apron uses soft cotton fabric 22″ long, 36″ wide; topstitch rows of embroidered novelty trims, bias tapes, and rickrack.

Sew lacy edge, double-fold bias trim to sides, bottom. Gather apron top 3″x17″ waistband, including 3″x30″ ties. Next, cut two 7¾″ diameter circles from cotton for pocket. Decorate one circle. Stitch lining to upper portion of each circle; sew circles together around bottom and sides; trim with lacy bias tape. Then cut two lengths of fabric 2″x8½″. Fold each lengthwise, sew outer edges, and turn out. Finally, sew one end of each pocket, other ends to waistband as shown for the hanging pocket.

Greek key design on apron has an old-world look that's rich and pleasing. To make this apron, use a ¾-yard length of terra-cotta colored cotton and cut according to your own pattern, if you have one designed with cascades of soft folds or pleats at the sides.

Make a 4″x16″ waistband with two 1¾″x 30″ ties. To begin, border the edge with two rows of black-on-white Greek key trim that's available at notions counters. Hem edges at the same time. Next, baste pleats at top edge; stitch waistband to top edge. Then, stitch ties at same time. To finish, sew two rows key braid trim to the ends of the ties. Press pleats.

APRONS WITH A FOREIGN FLAIR

Oriental look not bought in a shop

Wear it as an apron or an overskirt

An oriental touch is added to ivory-colored cotton apron designed by Ann Joselyn. To make apron, cut ¾ of a yard of fabric and make the darts in the upper sections as shown in photograph. Sew pocket linings in place on lower section; then topstitch the top edge in place on the upper section, with the needle point positioned in center. Topstitch the pocket section. Sew flat red bias tape trim around sides, bottom, and slit openings. Then, sew waistband sections together, inserting interfacing between them. Attach 2″x22″ ties at the sides and stitch the waistband to the apron. Slip-stitch frog closings to pockets.

An India-print throw makes good-looking apron that covers front, back fully. Two aprons can be made from one throw. Cut throw in half lengthwise; cut off width 4½″ deep from top to serve as waistband and ties. Trim off more if necessary for desired length. Fold under 6½″ at side border designs; topstitch to form pocket openings. Sew gold metallic trim to sides and bottom of apron. Take the previously cut cloth for waistband and ties, fold over lengthwise. Sew together, leaving an opening in the center for the waistband portion (about 25″). Gather top of the apron to fit the waistband opening.

FINE
FOR
GIFTS

You can make fashionable cover-ups for the cook and the gardener on your gift list. Trim them with simple embroidery stitches, or use some of the good-looking braids, tapes, rickracks that are available at notions counters.

Another good idea is to press on mending-tape designs. Keep the design outline clean-cut so work will go quickly. It just takes a few seconds to add decoration.

Coral-colored apron with petite floral design begins with a 36″ wide, 19½″ long rectangle of polished cotton. The selvages are used for sides of apron and the bottom has a 3″-wide hemline. The top gathers and attaches to a 15″-long waistband. The ties, 23″ in length, attach to the ends of the waistband and are hemmed by hand.

Royal blue feather stitching borders the ties and waistband, skirt, and pockets. It also connects the dainty flowers running across the waistband and creates stems for the flowers on pocket, hem, and tie ends. The eight flower petals are formed by easy lazy-daisy stitch. French knots are used to add detail to the flowers and around the flower shapes. Designer: Roena Clement.

Floral banded apron in blue was designed by Susan Wright. Any color combination you wish of cotton and embroidered tape would work just as effectively. The apron starts with a 34″ wide, 17¼″ long piece of satin-finished, ribbed cotton.

The rectangle has narrowly hemmed sides for skirt and is faced at lower edge to the right side with woven tape. Next, 7″x7″ pieces press under ¼″ on three sides and the top of right side is faced with woven tape. Pockets are then topstitched in place about 4¼″ down from the top.

Finally, top edge of skirt is shirred to 18″. Then a 72″ strip of woven tape is topstitched to wide bias tape back-to-back, leaving 18″ free at center of lower edge. The shirred skirt slips between both tapes, is topstitched to form waistband, ties.

Rich pink apron is beautified by the addition of design of rickrack. Rickrack selected for use contrasts in color, size. Use of both wave and standard-size trim makes the design more interesting, gives a different flair to the finished apron. Add rickrack to ties, too, if you wish.

The pink apron is cut in about ¾ of a circle of a cotton-dacron blended fabric—make it at least this full for best effect. The hem and sides are stitched narrowly. The waistband is machine-stitched to the skirt top and secures 3½″ wide ties.

Wave braid is machine-stitched across the waistband and in two rows repeating the skirt shape. One row of plain rickrack centers between wave braid rows to repeat the design line and to add contrast.

An innovation for the "weeding set"—an apron to protect knees and clothing. The brown apron shown above is cut 1¼ yard of 40″ wide heavy cotton. Waist measures 15″, tapering out to 19″ at hips. Legs are slit up 13″ with patches placed at knee position. Pockets measure 9½″x7½″ with ties that are 20¼″x2¾″. The apron is doubled and bound with bias tape. Knee designs are cut from iron-on patches.

Royal blue apron, created by Roena Clement, illustrates the skilled craftsmanship of an artist. Now that it's created, however, the design could be reproduced with a little effort by anyone who learns a few easy-to-do embroidery stitches.

Apron begins with a 38½″ wide, 28″ long piece of cotton broadcloth. The rectangle has 1½″ wide hems turned back on the sides, then the top of apron gathers to fit and attaches to the tapered waistband. Before the ends of the waistband secure, 26″ long hemmed ties are inserted. Next, the side hems are stitched and a 3″ lower hem folds under and is secured.

Finally, embroidery stitches are added for decoration. The feather stitch borders waistband and ties, the skirt, and the pockets. A chain stitch waves along ties, across the waistband, and on the pockets. It also forms outline for the flowers and leaves. Yellow French knots add accent.

Flared skirt shift, left, has a giant flower, fringe trim. This idea is easy to adapt. Just sew a plain-colored shift, then sketch flower shapes in pencil. Use double-fold bias tape to shape the flowers, then, machine-stitch them in place.

Add fringe in a contrasting color along the hemline for a high-style appearance.

FASHION IN THE TRIMMINGS

Open lace trim is effective for a hemline border. A linen or linen-like fabric will combine nicely with lace stripes along hemline of plain dress. The lace is stitched by machine after the dress is completed.

Two-tone dress has Venice lace edging for trim. Slip lace edging in the seam between bodice and skirt of empire waistline shift. White top with dark blue skirt gives a cool appearance. Top with a matching head scarf.

Basic shift can be trimmed with giant print flowers. Third dimension plays a part in design of contrasting fabric—flowers are padded. Rickrack outlines the print designs.

Venice lace trims the neckline of shift, right. For a cool, crisp effect, try this idea on a deep turquoise colored dress. The daisies are cut from Venice lace that is available in notion departments. Neckline can be high or scooped—both work well with this trimming idea.

For a change in costume, add a daisy-trimmed belt to match the dress. Use a fine running stitch to attach the trim to the dress and belt.

A three-tiered, fringe-trimmed dress will collect compliments. To use this idea, cut a plain-line shift into three pieces as drawing at left indicates. Use bold printed fabric in the center section and border it, top and bottom, with gay white fringe. Attach the fringe along seams of the tiers after dress is stitched. When you attach fringe in this manner you can easily add another kind of fringe or trim at a later time and not have to re-sew the dress. This fringe is easily removable.

PRETTY TRIMMINGS

There are dozens of trimming touches that can give an entirely different look to the most simple dress. Sometimes, it's only the effect of smart plaid or check used on the bias that turns a simple dress into one that's really original.

Or, you can use ribbon and embroidered braid alone or with lace edgings or rick-rack sewed along each edge to create the colorful effect you want. There is an endless variety of trimmings, all made up and ready to apply. Look for these embroidered motifs, braids, and bandings in the trimmings department. Cording, too, often is used as a trim on children's clothes. It is available in a variety of colors and textures, ready to sew. All give a favorite little girl's dresses a custom look.

Empire waistline dress adapts itself readily for a truly delightful look for a small girl's best dress. Here, we've suggested one style that might be tried, but there's no end to the variation possibilities. Take a trip to the pattern and fabric section of your local department store or to a special fabric shop and try finding "just the right" pattern for your favorite miss. Consider the alternatives of fabric and color combinations with crisp white eyelet ruffling before buying the dress pattern, materials.

To make this feminine dress, follow the directions on the pattern you choose. When the dress is completed, add row after row of fluffy white eyelet as the drawing above suggests. Be sure to allow for a bit of overlap to achieve a good effect. Add rows of eyelet until the entire area from the high waistline to the hemline is completely covered.

Finish the designer touch on dress by adding a colorful ribbon band and making a matching bow for hair. Make several sets in different colors.

An A-line dress would be beautified by addition of a petitely designed woven tape with hearts and flowers.

If you choose a design with a natural neckline, the trimming pictured on A-line dress above can be reproduced without change.

When selecting the dress pattern, fabric, and trim consider the size of child and her coloring. Once you get the supplies at home, a few hours of work will be all that's needed. Cut out and sew dress leaving hem unfinished. Form tailored bow of tape and hand-tack it to the dress. Pin streamers in place and stitch by hand. Put in the hem after these streamers are in position.

Play dress designed for 4- to 5-year-olds is a basic A-line style trimmed with set of numbers at hemline.

The neckline style will not matter with this idea—choose the pattern and fabric to suit the child and the season of the year.

Make dress according to the directions of the pattern. Leave neckline and the

sleeves, hemline unfinished. Bind all three with double-fold bias tape. Now shape numbers with the bias tape.

Some angles can be folded but others must be cut and tucked underneath. Applique the figures in place. A variation to consider: Use letters to spell out a name.

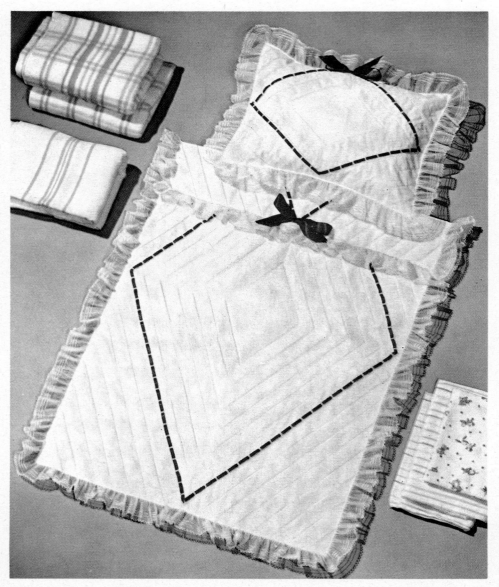

WARM DRESS-UPS

Felt robe, right, designed by Ann Joselyn, will make Baby warm and happy on his carriage outings. You'll need to buy 33x25½" strip felt, 1 yard flannelette for interfacing, 1 yard polished cotton lining, three 10x11" pieces different colored felt for the trim.

Pink edge of the piece of large felt. Trace flower designs on small pieces. Cut out neatly. Baste cutouts, cutout pieces on large felt. Fold under lining edges. Baste to felt with interlining between.

Sew all sections together, making border and outlining the cutouts.

Baby's carriage set, left, uses 2 yards of nylon organdy, one receiving blanket, 4 yards ½" ribbon, 1½ yards 1" ribbon, 5 yards nylon ruffling, 5 yards nylon beading. Pillowcase is 12½"x16½".

Cut two 24"x36" pieces organdy. Trim receiving blanket to same size. Using a yardstick, mark one layer nylon in diamond which nearly touches center of each outside edge. Rule six diamonds inside first, lines out to corners.

Pin three thicknesses together. Stitch on lines, sewing center triangle, working out. Run ribbon through beading; stitch on outside diamond on front side. Sew on back on same diamond 6" in from end.

Sew nylon ruffling around edge, right sides together. Turn, stitch. Fold down edge, add bow. Design: A. Wood.

Bedtime footwear, below, adjusts to fit growing feet. Cut paper pattern as shown, (1 square = 1 inch), for child's shoe sizes 7 to 9. Cut corduroy, cotton, flannelette for slippers. From cotton, make yard bias binding, 18" ties.

Baste flannelette between corduroy and cotton, right side out. Sew the binding around slipper. Sew on buttons as shown. Shape loops with four strands thread—blanket-stitch over them.

Make ⅝" buttonhole in tongue. Sew on 9" ties as in diagram. Slip these ties through slits and make bows at tops.

```
⊔ LOOP          BUTTON ⊕

↳ TIE                TIE ↲

◯ LOOP          BUTTON ⊕

              ▯ SLIT
```

Corduroy slippers, right, can be worn over pajamas. Loosen the bows to change size. Buy ¼ yard each corduroy, flannelette, striped cotton. You'll also need four buttons to complete the slippers.

Jingle-bell slippers, left, take ¼ yard of felt. In addition, you will need a set of felt soles for inside. Cut using scalloping shears. Fasten with grippers. Add felt soles inside. Design: E. Brown.

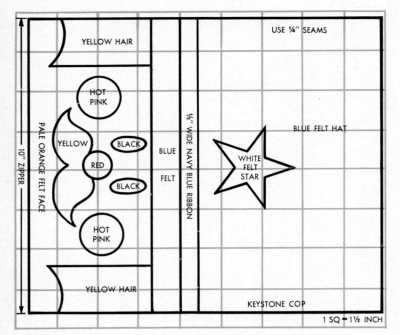

YELLOW HAIR

USE ¼" SEAMS

PALE ORANGE FELT FACE

10" ZIPPER

HOT PINK

YELLOW

BLACK

RED

BLACK

HOT PINK

BLUE FELT

½" WIDE NAVY BLUE RIBBON

BLUE FELT HAT

WHITE FELT STAR

YELLOW HAIR

KEYSTONE COP

1 SQ = 1½ INCH

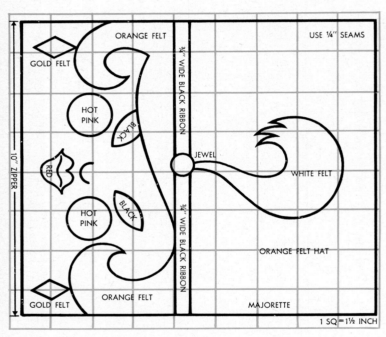

ORANGE FELT

USE ¼" SEAMS

GOLD FELT

¾" WIDE BLACK RIBBON

10" ZIPPER

HOT PINK

BLACK

RED

JEWEL

WHITE FELT

HOT PINK

BLACK

¾" WIDE BLACK RIBBON

ORANGE FELT HAT

GOLD FELT

ORANGE FELT

MAJORETTE

1 SQ = 1½ INCH

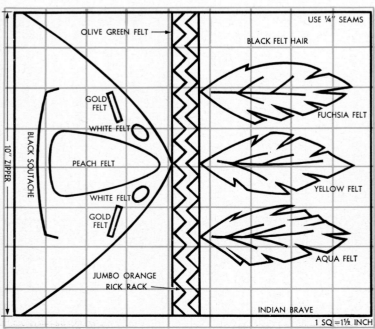

OLIVE GREEN FELT →

USE ¼" SEAMS

BLACK FELT HAIR

GOLD FELT

WHITE FELT

PEACH FELT

BLACK SOUTACHE

10" ZIPPER

FUCHSIA FELT

WHITE FELT

GOLD FELT

YELLOW FELT

JUMBO ORANGE RICK RACK

AQUA FELT

INDIAN BRAVE

1 SQ = 1½ INCH

PAJAMA PILLOWS OF FELT

Bright-colored, snappy pajama pillows for the youngsters in your family can be cut and stitched in a relatively short time. Try a solemn Indian brave design, a gay toy soldier, a drum majorette, or a keystone cop complete with mustache. Any caricatures of your own design could be made following the same method used for these. You'll need your scissors and sewing accessories, plus the glue pot and some thread, as well as pieces of felt and felt scraps in a variety of colors. Combine several colors on a single pillow to get a bright, poster effect.

The pillows shown here, designed by Mrs. Jackie Curry, begin with rectangles of felt and interfacing—two each—following the overall outline of the patterns. Each of the felt rectangles attaches to the interfacing. The hair, hat pieces, and features

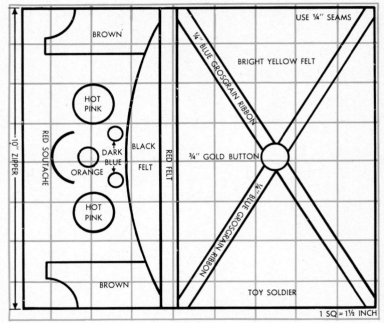

BROWN

USE ¼" SEAMS

¼" BLUE GROSGRAIN RIBBON

BRIGHT YELLOW FELT

RED SOUTACHE

10" ZIPPER

HOT PINK

DARK BLUE

BLACK FELT

ORANGE

RED FELT

¾" GOLD BUTTON

HOT PINK

¼" BLUE GROSGRAIN RIBBON

BROWN

TOY SOLDIER

1 SQ = 1½ INCH

attach to the face sections of the pillows with machine stitching. Finally, decorative trims such as rickrack, costume jewelry, and brass buttons are added. Either glue these trims, or, if you prefer, machine-stitch them to the face sections. Buttons, sequins, and similar details can be hand-tacked in place.

The same sequence for attaching features and trims to the fronts of the pillows is repeated on the back sides. You can design a back that continues the lines and colors used on the front, or, put a duplicate face on the back side.

The pillows open and close with zippers. The zippers machine-stitch to the bottom edge of the front and back pieces of the pillows. Then the zippers are opened and the pillows are completed by machine-stitching the remaining three sides of the front and back pieces together. Turn the pillows inside out to complete.

Sewing tip: A fine nylon thread is suitable for all sewing on these felt pillows. Using it helps eliminate the nuisance of the changing of bobbins and spools when you cross into new colors. The nylon thread absorbs the colors it adjoins and is also extra durable . . . which should help keep pillows in one piece during any possible pillow fights.

If you prefer, you can fill your caricature pillows with cotton or foam instead of leaving them empty for pajamas.

Energetic sewers may make a grouping of three or four pillows to toss on a bed.

Braun

COMPLETE

STITCHERY

Rocker cover, page 6. Cut pattern to fit pads you're covering. Seat and head portion are stuffed with kapok; backrest has foam-rubber pad. Lay pattern onto fabric; pin and cut. Next, cut out colored pieces of felt. Pin felt to background fabric; (place pins horizontally so you can sew over them).

Run average sewing stitch vertically back and forth over pieces to give textured effect. Seam three edges on reverse side, turn to right side; fill. Sew last edge by hand.

Wall hanging, page 7. Background is off-white nubby wool. Moss green leaf is cut of felt; basted to background. Cut flowers and leaves in felt and burlap; baste to green felt. If you have conventional sewing machine, remove presser foot and attach "darning foot." Put feeder teeth out of action. Set machine on "low" if you can.

If yours is a zigzag or fully automatic machine, set dial for "free motion." Use needle for medium to heavy fabric; use even tension for top and bobbin.

Starting at outer edge, machine-stitch each flower following design. Continue without cutting thread from flower to flower, ending with the stems.

Folding stool, page 8. Use fabric with an even or regular stripe. (If a random stripe is used, some stripes are kept flat with no stuffing. At other places, stuffed stripes occur next to each other.)

After lines have been stuffed with cording, edge cover with bias tape to match the fabric and stool colors. Tack into place on stool, or stitch trapunto fabric to an existing cover of the stool.

Print pillow, page 8. Fabric used was soft, synthetic kind with crepe surface, which is ideal for this kind of stuffing. Pillow is backed with a color relating to print.

Red burlap pillow, page 8. Cut two 17-inch squares of red burlap. Then cut one 11-inch square from pink for the applique. Cut bias strips to cover cording from pink burlap 1⅜ inches wide. Piece where necessary to make 65 inch length. Draw petals on pink burlap. Center and baste to one of the red squares; put cotton batting in between.

Satin-stitch around design. Closely trim away excess fabric. With open zigzag, stitch yarn in center of applique. Cut eight 7-inch lengths of yarn; zigzag each piece between petals of applique making three loops at each end. To cover cord with the bias strip, fold strip through center; press. Place the cord in fold; use adjustable cording zipper foot; stitch close to the cord (take ½-inch seam allowance.)

With raw edges even, pin and stitch cording to the right side of red square, notching the cording seam allowances at corners. Turn under; overlap raw edges at end of the cording. Place red squares with right sides together (raw edges even); pin. Stitch three sides. Turn cover to right side; insert the pillow. Turn free edges of opening to the inside; pin. Slip-stitch opening by hand.

Red throw, page 8. Cut backing fabric same size you wish your finished piece to be. It

DIRECTIONS

is best to have color match that of blocks.

Cut applique pieces from a variety of colors, keeping them in close range. (That is, cut an assortment of reds and oranges, or of blues and greens.)

Pin squares and rectangles in random arrangement over backing or use loose basting stitch. Then machine-baste with narrow zigzag (one of the newer model machines has a chain stitch to use for basting). Do final machine sewing using a decorative machine stitch which will cover basting stitch.

When all pieces are stitched to backing, draw star shapes in center of some blocks. Machine-stitch the star outlines with satin stitch. Edge throw with matching binding.

Sunshine pillow, page 8. Cut out two 15-inch circles of blue felt; one 5-inch circle of yellow for sun disk. Do not cut out rays. Draw them on gold felt; satin-stitch design on machine. Cut rays carefully so you don't cut the thread.

Place rays on top piece of felt; attach sun disk in center with decorative embroidery stitch. Insert round pillow; sew around edges, allow ½ inch seam. Pink edges.

Balloon pillow, page 8. Cut an 18-inch square piece of textured fabric, using half for front. Cut balloons and vendor from felt and applique with satin stitch. Run straight stitching line for each balloon thread. Sew pillow together; finish last side by hand.

Green pillow, page 8. Cut identical 11x17-inch rectangles of green fabric, yellow fabric. Cut out flowers, stems, from felt and applique on green fabric. Finish pillow.

Pink rectangular pillow, page 8. Cut two 10x18-inch pieces of felt. Cut irregular designs from both printed and plain cotton; applique with satin stitch. Cover with transparent nylon; stitch down with zigzag motif.

Round pink pillow, page 8. Cut three circles 15 inches in diameter; two from pink felt, one from transparent nylon. Cut three smaller circles, one pink, one wine, and one white felt. Cut these circles of felt round and round like peeling apple. Weave the cut pieces in and out. Place them on pillow top; cover with circle of nylon fabric. Stitch fabrics together in star pattern using embroidery stitch, many colors of thread.

Pillow and record carrier, page 9. Cut two 15-inch circles pink, two purple felt. Cut petals and flower centers. Attach to felt with embroidery stitch. For record carrier, line with plastic circles same size as felt.

Paper-doll quilt, page 9. Put ready-made quilt on bed. Baste edge where sides, bottom edge drop down. Measure to find center of quilt at bottom edge, mark. Cut out patterns (see outlines next page). Put quilt on floor. Position tissue patterns, putting center of one figure at center position on quilt, or let hands meet at this point. Cut out sail-cloth figures. Pin in place on the quilt, putting feet at lower edge. Baste with zigzag stitch at medium width, using matching thread. With thread matching each applique piece, sew over edge of pieces with satin stitch at full width. Press appliques.

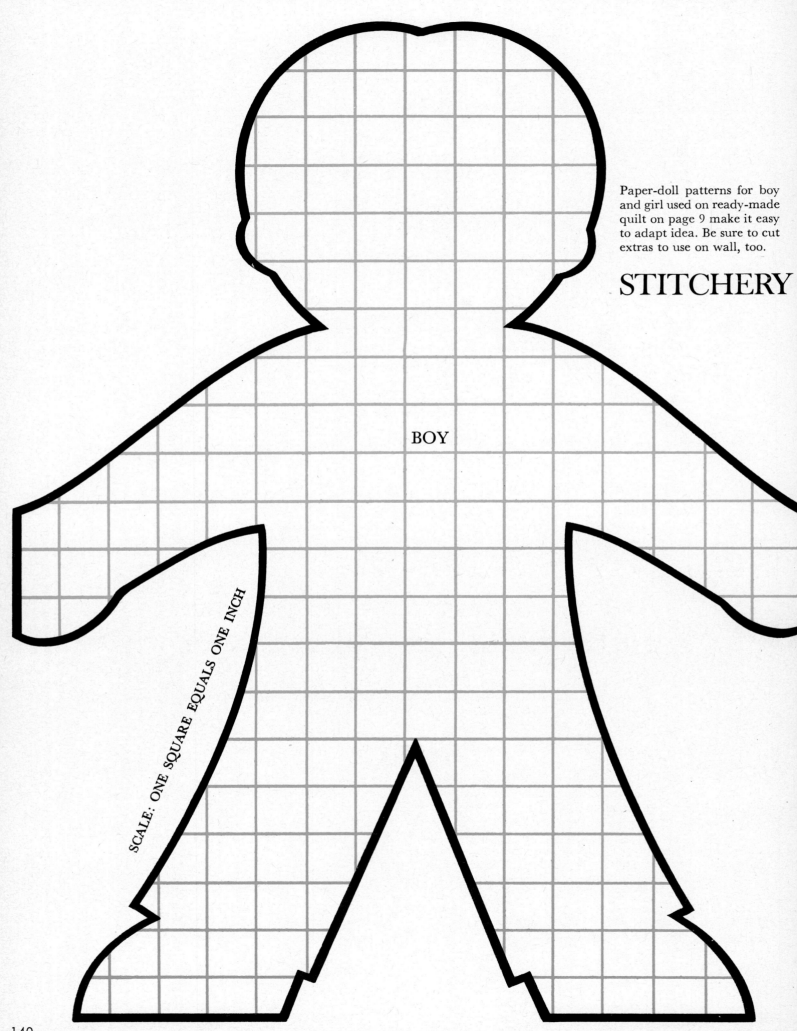

Paper-doll patterns for boy and girl used on ready-made quilt on page 9 make it easy to adapt idea. Be sure to cut extras to use on wall, too.

STITCHERY

BOY

SCALE: ONE SQUARE EQUALS ONE INCH

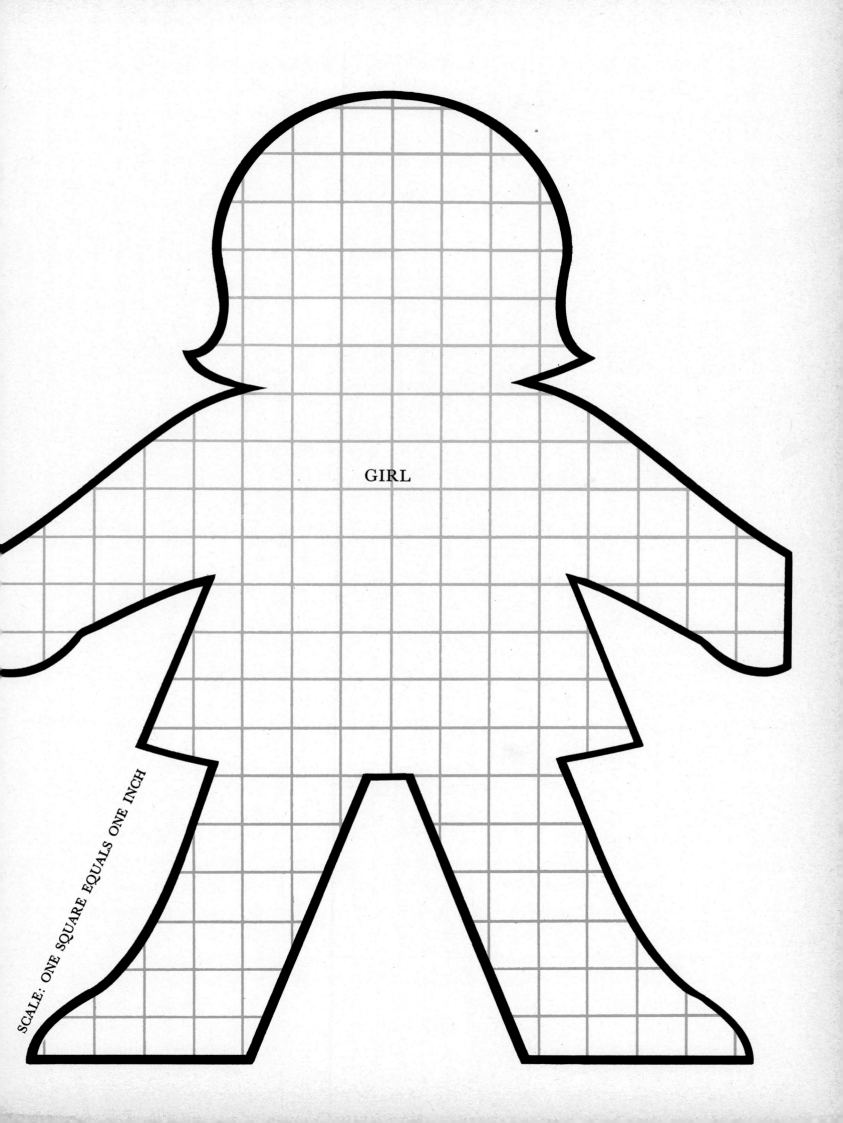

GIRL

SCALE: ONE SQUARE EQUALS ONE INCH

DESIGN D

DESIGN G

DESIGN C

DESIGN E

DESIGN J

CUT ON THIS EDGE

SCALE: ONE SQUARE EQUALS ONE INCH

Felt rug shown on page 11.

1 LIGHT YELLOW
2 YELLOW ORANGE
3 OFF-WHITE
4 DARK GREEN
5 LIGHT GREEN
6 RED
7 ORANGE

DESIGN M

DESIGN A

DESIGN B

DESIGN K

DESIGN F

DESIGN H

DESIGN L

DESIGN L

CUT ON THIS EDGE

ATTACH FRINGE ON THIS EDGE

CUT ON THIS EDGE

ACTUAL SIZE

Felt rug shown on page 11.

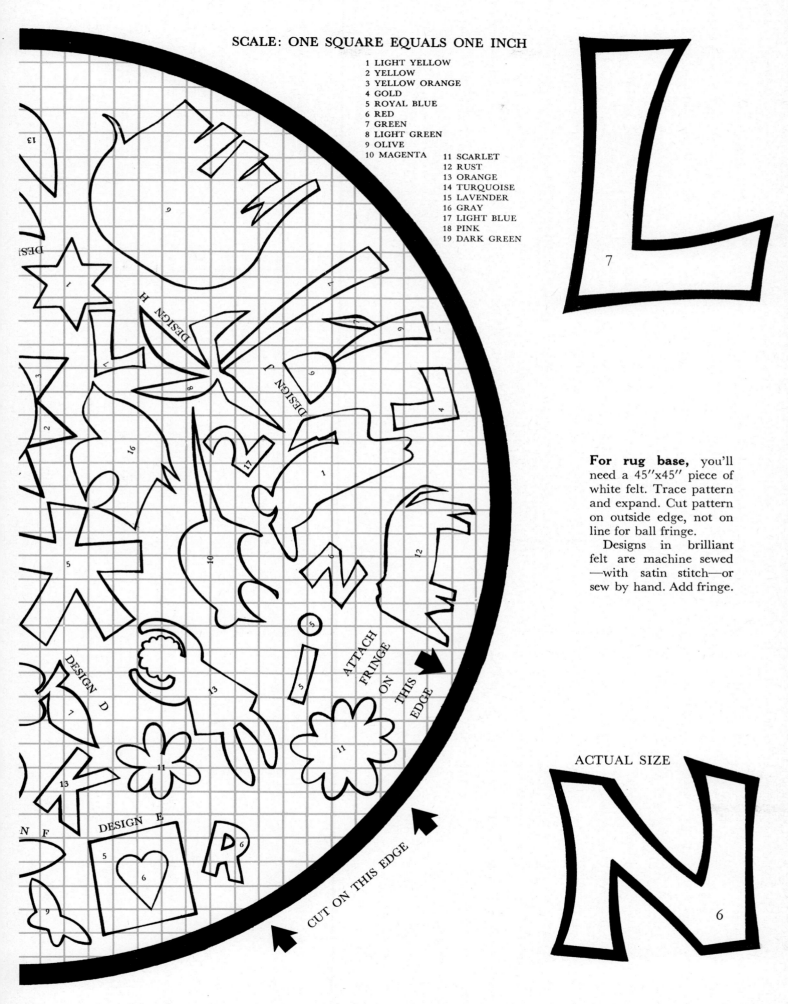

SCALE: ONE SQUARE EQUALS ONE INCH

1 LIGHT YELLOW
2 YELLOW
3 YELLOW ORANGE
4 GOLD
5 ROYAL BLUE
6 RED
7 GREEN
8 LIGHT GREEN
9 OLIVE
10 MAGENTA

11 SCARLET
12 RUST
13 ORANGE
14 TURQUOISE
15 LAVENDER
16 GRAY
17 LIGHT BLUE
18 PINK
19 DARK GREEN

ATTACH FRINGE ON THIS EDGE

CUT ON THIS EDGE

For rug base, you'll need a 45″x45″ piece of white felt. Trace pattern and expand. Cut pattern on outside edge, not on line for ball fringe.

Designs in brilliant felt are machine sewed —with satin stitch—or sew by hand. Add fringe.

ACTUAL SIZE

CROWN QUILT

Cutting layout crown quilt applique

Pattern for applique of crown quilt

For this quilt, you will need six pieces of light turquoise blue, six of an olive green, six of yellow, six of black, and six pieces of white.

Allow for a ¼-inch seam around the outside of the pieces as you cut them from the fabric.

Materials needed for the crown quilt

1. Cotton bedspread—plain color, single or double. If you are making the bedspread, use a close-textured cotton. Get 9½ yards of 36″ cotton.

2. For design applique—2 yards of sateen finish cotton in assorted colors, harmonious to bedspread color. (Photo shows bright blue bedspread with appliques of turquoise blue, light turquoise blue, olive, yellow, black, white.)

Each design unit is of two pieces of different colors. If you are using six colors, you will need ½ yard of each color.

3. You will need thread to match both the spread and the applique colors.

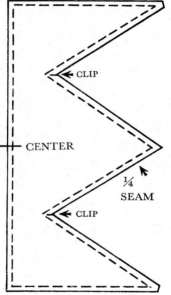

Instructions for the crown quilt

Bedspread

1. Double size—Cut 36″ wide material into three lengths of 1.13″ (3 yards, 5″) each. Cut one of the lengths into 22″ width.

For twin size, cut two lengths 113″x21″ width.

2. With ½″ seam, baste three lengths together—side by side—with narrower 22″ width in center.

3. Sew by machine, or by hand, using backstitch.

4. Cut two corners of fabric that will be bottom of bedspread, making gentle curve. (This makes a neat corner for draping on the bed).

5. By machine, or by hand using backstitch, make a ½″ hem all around.

Applique

1. Make pattern on heavy paper. This works better than tissue. Make several.

2. Pin patterns on fabrics selected, and cut. You'll need 36 pieces. There are 18 design units, each unit is made of two pieces of harmonizing or contrasting colors.

3. Place spread on a flat surface. From top center of spread measure down 5½ inches. Mark this spot by inserting pin.

4. Place two pieces of the applique horizontally, with center points meeting at spot marked. Turn

under edges ¼″, pin, and baste in place with the points of crowns meeting.

5. 3½″ to the right of this applique, line up two more pieces of applique; this time vertically, with points meeting. Turn under ¼.″ Pin and baste.

6. Repeat step 5, but to the left of center applique design.

7. Directly down from bottom of each applique design just placed, measure down 13″. Mark with pins. (The space above allows for tuck-in under pillow).

8. At spots marked, and in line with top three appliques, place three more design units, alternating horizontal and vertical placement—each design unit in this row measures 3½″ apart. (If bedspread is made as directed above, the center seams of bedspread can be used as the guides for lining up applique design—the inner edges of two outside design units placed on seams).

9. From bottom of row of appliques just placed, measure down 2¼″. Repeat step 8.

10. Continue from step 9 until there are six rows in all (including top row above pillow turn-under) of three design units in each row.

11. Machine-stitch designs.

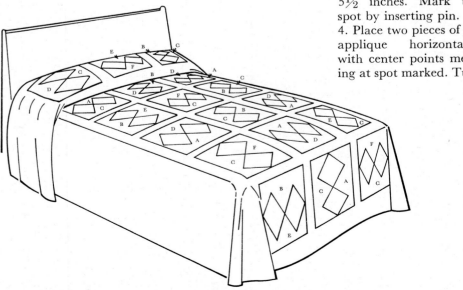

A Light turquoise blue

B Turquoise blue

C Olive green

D Yellow

E Black

F White

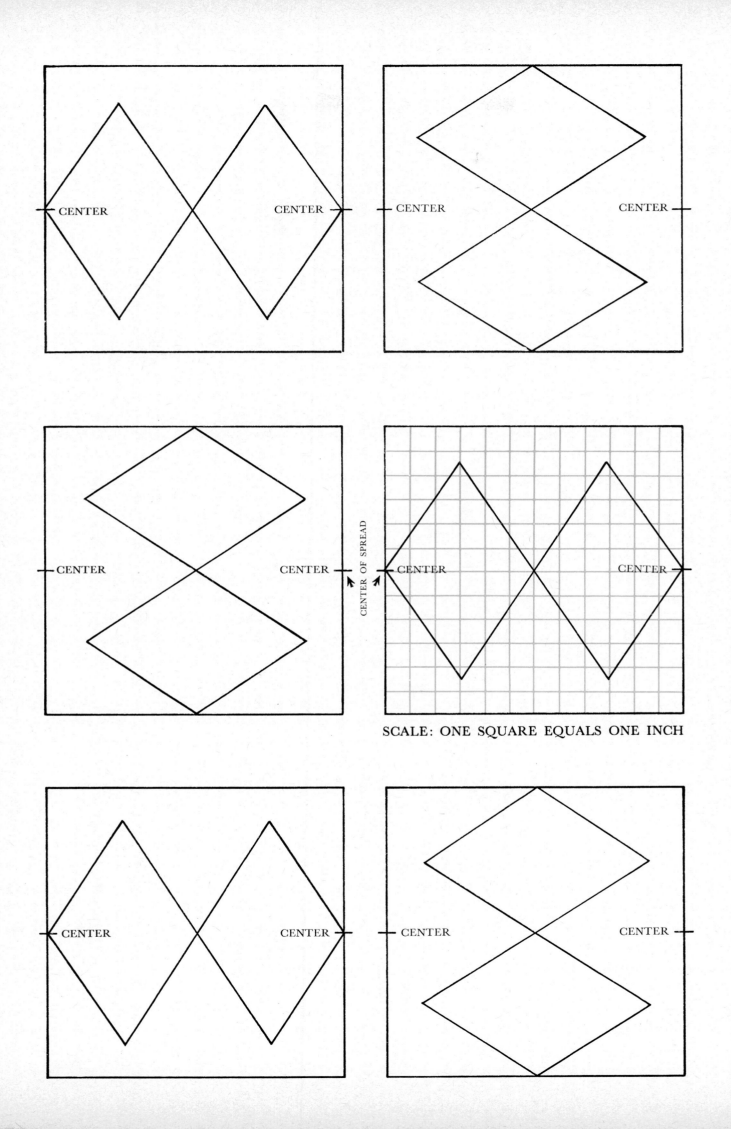

SCALE: ONE SQUARE EQUALS ONE INCH

SHORTCUTS FOR QUILTERS

The first step in determining the amount of fabric needed for the project you intend to make is to decide on the width of the strips and the number of colors.

Next, measure over your bed with a tape measure to help you visualize the total. Decide, too, on how much overhang is needed on the bed.

Suppose you decide that your quilt is to measure $5\frac{1}{2}$x$7\frac{1}{2}$ feet, as the one pictured does. You should start with about seven yards of 36-inch fabric. This should be divided among the six or so colors you expect to use, so that the shade to be emphasized predominates. The accent and auxiliary colors are used in proportionate amounts to the primary one selected.

The important thing is to keep all strips the same width. (Finished width of the strips in the quilt is about $1\frac{1}{8}$ inches after a seam allowance of $\frac{1}{4}$ inch on each side.) It is best to divide strips evenly into the width of the fabric. This eliminates any waste when you get to the edge of it.

After pieces are cut, varying from four to twelve inches in length, place them in a large box or basket; stir well. Plucking them at random from the box, start machine-stitching pieces together (never sew two in the same color next to each other), first in twos, then into fours, and next into long strips. Roll each long strip onto a cardboard roller just as tape is rolled. After you have a quantity of strips in a roll, cut two in the width your quilt is to be. Look them over and see that the colors, and where they are joined, fall in different places. Next, seam them together, being careful not to draw one tighter than the other one as they go through the sewing machine. Keep the little joining seams flat. Continue sewing them together until the quilt is the desired length. Of if you find it less cumbersome, make the top in several crosswise sections before machine-stitching them together. Press all crosswise seams open, and your top is ready to assemble and quilt.

For a backing, you will need two widths of a harmonizing fabric with your quilt top. Cut it a little longer than the quilt top. Join two lengths together; press center seam open. Use a cotton flannel blanket, or cotton or dacron batt, as filler. Spread backing, wrong side up on floor; center filling over it. Spread quilt top right side up over filler. Allow at least $1\frac{1}{2}$ inch of backing to extend all around for possible later adjustment.

Use basting stitches to temporarily position the 3 layers together, or use medium-size safety pins, as they can be easily moved or adjusted, if necessary. Whether you pin or baste, begin in the center of the quilt and work toward the outside. Start first along the vertical axis, then the horizontal axis. If pinning, place pins at 6-inch intervals. Continue pinning or basting in parallel lines on either side of each axis until quilt is completed.

The quilting is simple and easy to do. Choose a single color of thread that harmonizes with all the piecing colors and use it throughout. Use single or double thread as you prefer. Begin quilting at the center of the quilt, working out in all directions. Each block of the piecing is quilted with small, even stitches about $\frac{1}{8}$ inch inside seams.

For tiny stitches, make each one in two motions—first, straight down through the fabric; the next, straight back up. Generally the space between stitches, as seen from the top, should be somewhat longer than the length of the stitch itself.

If working without a quilting frame, it is best to pass the needle in and out of the fabric in a single movement. This allows the fabric to hump upward a bit where the needle is under it and the stitch is sure to go completely through all layers. Make only one stitch at a time to produce the slightly rippled effect so characteristic of quilting.

After entire top is quilted, run a careful, straight line of machine stitching around the quilt; trim evenly. Complete edge with bias binding the same color as backing; cut about $1\frac{1}{2}$ inch wide. This will finish to about a $\frac{1}{2}$-inch border. Or if enough backing has been left all around, it can be folded toward front and whipped down to make a $\frac{1}{2}$-inch finished hem as a border for your quilt.

After quilting, trim with ball fringe to match the predominant color, if desired. You can also make a gathered dust ruffle and a bolster in the same solid color to complete your new bedspread ensemble.

Quilting for the screen, chair, wastebasket, and vanity stool cover uses the same process.

CROCHETING

CHAIN STITCH: This is the simplest and most basic stitch. Make a slip-knot on hook. Pass hook under thread. Catch thread, draw it up through loop on hook making new loop for desired length.

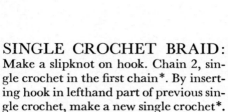

SINGLE CROCHET BRAID: Make a slipknot on hook. Chain 2, single crochet in the first chain*. By inserting hook in lefthand part of previous single crochet, make a new single crochet*. Continue, repeating from * to *.

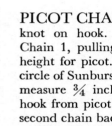

PICOT CHAIN: Make a slip-knot on hook. *Chain 4, then Chain 1, pulling loop to desired height for picot. (Those on outer circle of Sunburst pillow, page 22, measure ¾ inch high.) Remove hook from picot loop; insert it in second chain back. Draw yarn up making new stitch; repeat from *.

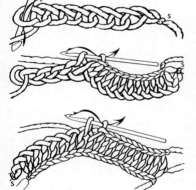

LADDER BRAID: Use cotton or wool rug yarn; divide it into two balls. Using a large wooden rug-crocheting needle, make a very loose chain with loops that measure ¾ inches long. Don't cut yarn. (Notice there are single loops on one side of chain, crossed loops on the other.) With other ball of yarn and No. 6 needle, beginning at single loop side of first chain, make a slip stitch through each loop until entire chain has been worked. Chain will shorten up; make more if it's necessary. Now work back down other side of chain. This time make slip stitches through point where loops intersect. While you are working second side, give a little pull sideways to original chain. Threads in between should spiral around each other making the ladder.

GLUE DESIGNS IN PLACE. Adhesive to use depends upon the fabric—whether it's to be laundered or dry-cleaned. White glues, sold at stationery counters (sometimes labeled "polyvinyl acetate emulsion") have excellent adhering qualities for fabric to be dry-cleaned, but can't be laundered. Others, with a latex-based composition, labeled "fabric glues," (found at notions counters) are guaranteed washable, but can't be cleaned.

Work with waxed paper under fabric to catch any adhesive that might leak through. If you are gluing to fabric for the first time, you'll find it easier to pour a small amount of glue into

a saucer, then apply it to fabric with a fine paintbrush or cotton swab. Spread a thin line (about 3 or 4 inches at a time) along design. Don't rub glue into fabric. Place crocheted trim in place; pat down firmly. Don't stretch or pull crochet; let it fall along the line gently to avoid puckering fabric underneath. When there is an abrupt change of direction in line, hold trim in place with pin for a few minutes to set.

DRAPERY: On plain paper, draw design using cup or bowl as pattern. Make corner and about 2 feet of running border, which can be repeated for desired length. To transfer design to fabric: Place pattern over fabric on slightly spongy surface such as carpet; stab through paper pattern with ball-point pen in dots about ¼ inch apart. If fabric is sheer, place fabric over pattern, then dot with pen directly on fabric. For fringe, use a soft, bulky yarn. One 2-ounce skein makes about 2 yards when worked over a 1½-inch width of wood, such as a wooden ruler.

FRINGE: Crochet chain about as long as fringe needed. Don't cut yarn until you're sure how much is needed. With another ball of yarn, begin at start of chain. Make starting loop on hook. Insert hook in first chain, wrap yarn behind and around stick. Pull yarn through chain and loop as you would a slip stitch. For heavy fringe, make two such loops in each chain. Allow fringe to slide off stick. When gluing fringe on, twist alternately left and right a half turn. Loops of fringe always radiate out from curves.

DIVIDER PANEL: If panel will be seen from both sides and fabric is sheer, use two lengths, each measuring 50x90 inches. Glue motifs on front; second length is lining (or glue motifs on both sides). On heavy fabric, adhesive won't show through.

For motifs, use a bulky homespun yarn which is spun with alternating thick and thin places about every 3 inches. With a No. 6 or G hook, Chain 16, turn. Insert hook in last chain from hook. Reach for first thin spot in yarn, allowing the heavy 3 inches between to form a loop on back side. Pull yarn through; complete stitch as single crochet. Repeat, working a single crochet in each chain stitch with a 3-inch loop of yarn between each one (15 loops in all). Turn, single crochet across. Repeat these 2 rows as many times as specified below.

To make row of long fringe-like loops: Skip first thin place in yarn; reach for a second one about 6 inches down yarn. Make a single crochet as before, but with a loop twice as long between each one. Rows on divider are placed 10 inches apart; motifs are graduated in size. *For bottom two rows,* motifs start with a chain of 16 with 3 rows of 3-inch loops and 1 row of 6-inch loops. *Rows 3 and 4:* Start with a chain of 14; have two rows of 3-inch loops, and one row of 6-inch loops. *Rows 5 and 6:* Start with a chain of 12; have one row of 3-inch loops, and one row of 6-inch loops. *Rows 7 and 8:* Start with a chain of 10 and a row of 6-inch loops.

PILLOWS

Sunburst pillow: Using cotton rug yarn, make about 2 yards of Chain Stitch crochet. Start at pillow center; glue chains in circles. Make length of Picot Chain to go outside of circle.

Abstract designed pillow: This is more or less like a doodle. Make large chain by combining several strands of yarn in close vibrant shades. Place it directly on pillow until you get a composition you like. Glue in place.

Intersecting arcs: With a compass draw design on paper to fit size of pillow. Transfer design to pillow as suggested for drapery. Using colors you choose, Chain-stitch any 4-ply yarn.

Striped pillow: This design uses a series of Chain Stitch, Single Crochet Braid, Ladder Braid, and Picot Chain. They were done in cotton rug yarn, mounted on green pillow cover.

Knitting instructions for items that are shown on page 20.

Knitting abbreviations

k . . . . knit
p . . . . purl
st(s) . . . . stitch(es)
sl . . . . slip
tog . . . . together
psso . . . . pass slipped stitch over
rnd . . . . round
dp . . . . double-pointed needle
yo . . . . yarn over
rem . . . . remaining
m . . . . knitting two stitches into one

yo 2 reversed; wrap yarn backward over needle twice
( ) Repeat instructions within ( ) as many times as specified outside ( )
* Repeat whatever follows the * as many times as specified

CHAIR SEAT COVER

Materials
Foam rubber for cushion: app. 1 yard, ⅝ inches thick.
Yarn:
4 ply knitting worsted, Amethyst, app. 1 ounce
4 ply knitting worsted, Skipper Blue, app. 1 ounce
4 ply kntiting worsted, Dark Turquoise, app. 1 ounce
4 ply knitting worsted, Black, app. 8 ounces
Mercerized crochet cotton, Skipper Blue, 1 ball
Mercerized crochet cotton, Parakeet, 1 ball
Mercerized crochet cotton, Nu-purple, 1 ball
Mercerized crochet cotton, Black, 2 balls
No. 6 knitting needle or size to get the correct gauge
GAUGE: 4½ sts = 1 in. blocked

DIRECTIONS: Cast on with black cotton and wool together 76 sts. K 1 row. P 1 row. Repeat 3 times. K 3 sts in black, (k 6 sts in blue, sl 2 black) repeat ( ) ending with 6 blue, add black and k 3. P 3 black, (p 6 blue, sl 2 black) re-

peat ( ) p 3 black. Repeat the above 2 rows 3 times. With black only, k 1 row, p 1 row. K 3 black, change to turquoise, k 2, (sl 2 black, k 6) repeat ( ) k 2 turquoise, k 3 black. P across keeping pattern and color. Repeat above 2 rows 3 times. With black only, k 1 row, p 1 row.

Amethyst row is same as blue row. There are 13 color rows ending in blue.

With black only, k 1 row, p 1 row. At the beginning of next 2 rows cast off 10 sts. At beginning of next 2 rows cast off 15 sts, cast off remaining sts.

Block to paper pattern that is the shape of chair seat. It should be ¼ inch bigger all the way around to accommodate the height of the foam.

A row of single crochet across the top will make the curve more even.

BACK: Cast on 76 sts, k 1 row, p 1 row, until back is the same size as the front and shape the top the same way and block back; knit with black mercerized crochet cotton and worsted.

TIES: Single crochet with wool and cotton together to make ties. You'll need four 9-inch ties for each cushion. Stitch ties in place to secure cushion to chair.

PLACEMAT

Finished blocked size: 13 in. x 19 in.
Materials
Blue (10/2) linen hand-weaving yarn. Amount needed for 8 mats, 4 spools.
No. 7 needle or size for gauge
GAUGE: 4 sts = 1 in. blocked

DIRECTIONS: Cast on 53 sts with two strands of linen (loosely). K 1 row, p 1 row, repeat this 8 times for border. K 3 sts * yo, k 2 tog * repeat across, k last 2 sts. P across row. Repeat these 2 rows 5 times. K 1 row, p 1 row. K 3 sts, * yo, k 2 tog * repeat across, k last 2 sts. P across row. Repeat these 2 rows 5 times. K 1 row, p 1 row, repeat 2 times. K 3 sts yo, k 2 tog * repeat across, k last 2 sts. P across row. Repeat these 2 rows 5 times. K 1 row, p 1 row, k 1 row, p 1 row. K 3 sts, * yo, k 2 tog * repeat across, k last 2 sts. P across row. Repeat these 2 rows 5 times. K 1 row, p 1 row. K 3 sts, * yo, k 2 tog * repeat

across, k last 2 sts. P across row. Repeat these two rows 5 times. K 1 row, p 1 row 8 times, cast off.

To block: Use heavy wrapping paper and mark off by inches an area 13 in. x 19 in.; leave extra paper on all sides. Use a piece of wallboard or cork to put the paper on top of. Dampen the mat completely and get out excess moisture with a towel. Before beginning to pin with extra heavy pins, stretch the mat in both directions. Pin every inch on all sides and then every half inch to keep the edges straight. A small amount of starch will give the mats more body.

HANGING LIGHT FIXTURE COVER

Materials
Fixture: White single pendant 8 inches in diameter and 13 inches long
Yarn: ½ pound bleached slub linen
Dp long No. 10 knitting needle or size for proper gauge
Markers
GAUGE: 4 sts = 1 in. 5 rows = 1 in. blocked

DIRECTIONS: Cast on 78 sts. Divide to three needles. *1st section:* * sl 1, k 1, psso, k 7, m 1 into next st (k first into front and then into back before slipping it off the needle); put on marker, k 3 * repeat. K 1 rnd. K these two rows 8 times. *2nd section:* * m 1 (k into front and then into back of st), k 7, sl 1, k 1, psso, put on marker, k 3 * put on marker, repeat. Knit 1 rnd. *3rd section:* same as 1st section. *4th section:* same as 2nd section, except there are only 7 repeats. At the beginning of 8th repeat sl 1, k 1, psso, k 7, sl 1, k 1, psso, repeat. Cast off.

To finish: Put knit piece on the plastic and slightly draw the ends over and into the shade; secure the ends tightly. Dip the whole shade into warm water. If the shade has become slightly soiled put a little soap and bleach into the water. Put several strings through the holes and hang up to dry. Install.

HAND KNIT PILLOW
14 in. x 14 in.

Materials

Yarn: Mercerized crochet cotton, Parakeet, 2 spools
4 ply knitting worsted, Green, 5 ounces
No. 7 knitting needle or size to obtain the right gauge
Marker
GAUGE: 4 sts = 1 in. blocked

FRONT: Cast on 53 sts with cotton and wool, k 1 row, p 1 row.

DIRECTIONS: *1st row:* k 2, put on marker. This is the beginning of every odd row. The pattern directions start after the marker. K 1 * yo, sl 1, k 1, psso, k 7, k 2 tog, yo, k 1 * repeat * to *, put on marker, (k 2 end of odd row). *2nd row:* all even rows are p. *3rd row:* k 1 * yo, k 1, sl 1, k 1, psso, k 5, k 2 tog, k 1 yo, k 1 * repeat * to * k 2. *5th row:* k 1 * yo, k 2, sl 1, k 1 psso, k 3, k 2 tog, k 2, yo, k 1 * repeat * to * k 2. *7th row:* k 1 * yo, k 3, sl 1, k 1, psso, k 1, k 2 tog, k 3, yo, k 1 * repeat * to * k 2. *9th row:* k 1, * yo, k 4, sl 1, k 2 tog, psso, k 4, yo, k 1 * repeat to * k 2. *11th row:* k 1 * k 3, k 2 tog yo, k 1, yo, sl 1, k 1, psso, k 4 * repeat * to * k 2. *13th row:* k 1 * k 2, k 2 tog, k 1, yo, k 1, yo, sl 1, k 1, psso, k 3 * repeat * to * k 2. *15th row:* k 1 * k 1, k 2 tog, k 2, yo, k 1, yo, k 2, sl 1, k 1, psso, k 2 * repeat * to * k 2. *17th row:* k 1 * k 2 tog, k 3, yo, k 1, yo, k 3, sl 1, k 1, psso * k 1 * repeat * to * k 2. *19th row:* k 2 tog * k 4, yo, k 1, yo, k 4, sl 1, k 2 tog, psso * repeat * to * ending k 4, sl 1, k 1, psso k 2.

Repeat the above pattern four times ending with a p row and then cast off.

BACK: Cast on 56 sts, k 1 row, p 1 row. Continue until the back is the same size as the front.

Blocking: Block to 14½ inches.

Putting together: Use a single crochet st working with the pattern side of pillow toward you.

Pillow lining: Make the lining of the pillow of cotton to match the crochet cotton color.

HAND KNIT PILLOW
11 in. x 11 in. with 1½ in. boxing

Materials

Yarn: 4 ply knitting worsted, Peacock, 4 ounces
Twisted embroidery thread, light Emerald Green, 4 balls
No. 7 knitting needle or size to obtain the right gauge
Marker
GAUGE: 4 sts = 1 in. blocked

FRONT: Cast on 46 sts with cotton and wool, k 1 row, p 1 row.

DIRECTIONS: *1st row:* k 2, put on marker. P 2 * keep yarn in front and sl 1 yarn to the back and k 2 tog, psso, yo 2 reversed to make 2 sts on needle. P 2 * marker, k 2. *2nd row:* p 2, k 2 * p 1, k 1, into over, p 1, k 2, * repeat * to *, marker ending in p 2. *3rd row:* k 2 * p 2, k 3 * repeat * to *, ending in p 2, k 2. *4th row:* p 2, k 2, * p 3, k 2, * repeat * to *, ending in p 2. Repeat the 4 pattern rows 12 times; do the first 2 rows of the pattern. K 1 row, p 1 row, cast off.

BACK: Cast on 42 sts, k 1 row, p 1 row, repeat until piece is the same size as the front. The pillow can be made completely reversible.

Blocking: Block front and back piece to 11¼ inches.

SIDE PIECE: Cast on 6 sts, k 1 row, p 1 row for 10¾ inches, k 3 rows, * (Repeat three times to make four sides); cast off. Block 1½ inches wide and each section 11¼ inches long.

Putting together: Single crochet the front piece to the side piece being sure that the ridge is at the corners; single crochet the back piece to the sides leaving enough room to slip in the pillow before finishing.

Inside lining: Make a covering for the pillow of any plain cotton material that matches the green cotton yarn.

HAND KNIT PILLOW
13 in, x 19 in.
Materials

Yarn: 4 ply knitting worsted, Emerald Green, 1 ounce
4 ply knitting worsted, Skipper Blue, 4 ounces
4 ply knitting worsted, Dark Turquoise, 1 ounce
Mercerized crochet cotton, Black, 2 balls
Mercerized crochet cotton, Hunters Green, 1 ball
Mercerized crochet cotton, Parakeet, 1 ball
1 pair No. 7 knitting needles
GAUGE: 4 sts = 1 in. blocked.

FRONT: Cast on 50 sts with black cotton and blue wool. K 1 row, p 1 row loosely.

DIRECTIONS: *1st row:* k 1, put on marker, p 2 * yo, sl 2, p 2 pass the 2 slipped stitches over * repeat * to * ending p 2, k 1. *2nd row:* p 1, k 2, * k 1 (k 1, p 1, k 1) into over * repeat * to * ending in k 2, p 1. *3rd row:* k. (Knit this row loosely.) Repeat above three rows three times, p 1 row. Change to green wool and turquoise cotton and repeat above pattern. Change to blue wool and black cotton and repeat above pattern. Change to turquoise wool and green cotton and repeat above pattern. Change to blue wool and black cotton and repeat above pattern. Change to green wool and turquoise cotton and repeat above pattern. Change to blue wool and black cotton and repeat above pattern. Change to turquoise wool and green cotton and repeat above pattern. P 1 row. Cast off on knitting row.

BACK: Cast on 50 sts with black cotton and blue wool. K 1 row, p 1 row until the back of the pillow is the same size as the front.

Blocking: Block front and back to 13½ x 19½ inches.

Inside cover of pillow: Use blue cotton for the back. For the front make a stripe-cover using green cotton behind the turquoise and green stripe, turquoise cotton behind the green wool and turquoise cotton.

To put the pillow together: Use a single crochet st while you are holding the front of the pillow toward you. Work, using the black cotton and blue wool.

Pattern for wood mounting
frames used on wall hanging.

KNITTING

Left side of wall hanging goes on broken line.　　　21 in.　　　Right side of wall hanging goes on broken line.

1 ⅝ in.

Knitting instructions for afghan, wall hanging, wall light fixture cover shown on page 21.

Knitting abbreviations

k.............knit
p.............purl
st(s)..........stitch(es)
sl.............slip
tog...........together
psso..........pass slipped stitch over
rnd..........round
dp...........double-pointed needle
yo...........yarn over
rem..........remaining
m...........knitting two stitches into one

Yo 2 reversed; wrap yarn backward over needle twice.

( ) Repeat instructions within ( ) as many times as specified outside ( ).

* Repeat whatever follows the * as many times as specified.

AFGHAN

Materials
Yarn:
Mohair, Castilian Coral, 16 1-ounce balls
Twist Knitting worsted, Rust, four 4-ounce skeins
No. 11 needle 29 in. round or size to get the proper gauge
Blanket is knit 65 inches long and is knit 48 inches, instead of knitting 48 inches wide and 65 inches long. The rib is widthwise instead of lengthwise.

GAUGE: app. 2½ sts = 1 in.

DIRECTIONS: Cast on loosely 176 sts on a rnd needle 29 in. long, size 11, or size to get the correct gauge. Using Twist worsted k 1 row. P 1 row. Change to Mohair. *1st row:* (preparation row only) * yo, sl 1 purl-wise), k 1 * repeat. *2nd row:* * yo, sl 1 (purl-wise), k 2 tog * repeat. *3rd & 4th rows:* same as 2nd row. Change to Twist worsted and repeat 2nd row, four times. Repeat the above until 13 balls of Mohair are used, save the other 3 for the fringe. K 1 row, p 1 row with Twist worsted and cast off. To make a firm edge for the fringe loosely pick up 176 sts with Twist worsted and cast off. Do this at

the beginning and end of blanket. At the other two edges pick up sts with Twist worsted, 4 sts for every 8 rows of pattern (2 sts in the Mohair row, 2 sts in the Twist worsted row). K 1 row, p 1 row 3 times. K 3 rows, p 1 row, k 1 row, p 1 row, k 1 row, p 1 row, k 1 row, p 1 row, cast off. Turn back and hem.

Block: Fringe goes down the sides and is made with 3 strands Mohair, 1 strand Twist worsted 12 in. long.

WALL HANGING 21 in. x 76 in.

Materials
Yarn:
½ lb. wide raffia—shiny
No. 11 knitting needles

GAUGE: 2½ sts = 1 in., 3 rows = 1 in.

DIRECTIONS: Cast on 46 sts. K 1 row. P 1 row. The next two rows are repeated 90 times for a panel without wooden end pieces that measures 19 in. x 72 in. *1st row:* K 2, * lift 4th st over 3rd st and knit it, then knit 3rd st * repeat * to *, k 2. *2nd row:* P. Cast off knitting.

To Block: Use fiberboard or any other surface that it is possible to pin into. Mark heavy wrapping paper off in one section 20 in. x 74 in. Use heavy "T" pins that are sold at stationery stores. Put the straw into water and roll damp dry in a towel.

Before beginning to pin, pull the piece lengthwise and a little widthwise. Pin every inch at each end and then the sides. The more pins used after the first pinning the straighter the panel will be. Be very careful not to pin into the straw or it will tear. Spray with a satin finish spray or any plastic spray to give the hanging more body. (This is a good pattern for placemats, using a plain edge on each side.)

How to make mounting frames: Make pattern following guide on opposite page. Cut four pieces of quarter-inch hardwood 21 in. x 1⅝ in. Lay pattern over front board. Punch through center of each circle on pattern with pin or nail for drill guide. Lay two boards together and drill holes with ½ inch drill through both pieces of wood.

On back side, glue ¾ in. piece of ½ in. dowel into each of the ten holes. Loop wall hanging onto each of the ten dowel pieces before adding the front piece. (Front piece is removable so that back piece can be nailed to wall.)

Repeat above steps on other end.

WALL LIGHT FIXTURE COVER

Materials
Fixture is white, measures 4 in. x 4 in. x 15 in.
Yarn: One bobbin each of the following:
7/1 White linen
10/1 Natural linen
White slub linen
Gold twist
Needles: No. 9 long dp

GAUGE: 3 sts = 1 in., measure stretched lace part

DIRECTIONS: Cast on with linen and metallic loosely 44 sts; leave at least 18 in. of yarn for finishing. Divide onto 3 needles.

PATTERN STITCH: * yo, k 2 tog * repeat * to *. *1st round:* * sl 1, k 1, psso, k first into front and then into back of st, put on marker, k 8, put on marker * repeat * to *. *2nd round:* k.

Pattern begins: *1st row:* sl 1, k 1, psso, k first into front and then into back of st, * yo, k 2 tog * repeat * to * 4 times and continue this sequence until one rnd has been made. *2nd row:* k. *3rd row:* change to slub linen and repeat the above 2 rows. The four rows are to be repeated 16 times. To end use metallic and linen: * sl 1, k 1, psso, k 8, * repeat * to * for one rnd. Cast off loosely.

To finish: Slip the shade onto the lamp at the beginning, keeping the bias sections at the four corners. Pull carefully but firmly until shade is stretched enough to fit over the four corners at other end. With extra yarn that was left at the finishing point, stitch in and out and pull in slightly so shade will not fall off. If it is too difficult to get the shade on, dampen it slightly. After shade is on, immerse it in hot water and hang up to dry. The lamp can be cleaned this way.

RABBIT DESIGN APPLIQUE

Materials needed

You'll need a pillowcase, sheet, washcloth, hand towel, bath towel. Choose contrasting colors for applique design. Any soft fabric appliques well. In addition, have on hand iron-on interfacing for use under the applique fabric, plus thread matching color of appliques.

Sheet

When sheet is appliqued, designs will cover entire width of the sheet; patterns are centered along top hem area of the sheet. For sheet you will need on the left half designs C, D, A, E, F, C, F, E in that order. In the center, use design A. For right half of sheet, use designs B, C, A, B, C, E, D, C in that order. Repeat steps 2, 3 under pillowcase.

Cut out patterns; cut required number of designs. Repeat steps 5, 6, 7 that are given under the pillowcase to finish the sheet.

Pillowcase

1. Trace designs full size for patterns. For a pillowcase, you'll need designs B, C, F, A, E, F to be put on pillowcase in that order. Each design will be centered along the hem area of the pillowcase.
2. Rabbit designs face both right and left. Trace as patterns indicate. When cutting, be sure to place the applique patterns on the right side of the fabric you use.
3. Apply iron-on interfacing to the wrong side of the fabric to be appliqued. The added stiffening will make machine appliqueing easier.

4. Cut out applique patterns, marking the pattern tops so you don't get them reversed.
5. Place patterns on applique fabric reinforced with interfacing. Draw around patterns. Cut, following the drawn line.
6. Pin each design in place on pillowcase following listed order. Do all of first design before proceeding to the other designs.
7. With thread matching each applique piece, machine-stitch, using satin stitch around each piece. When appliques are stitched, press with iron.

Bath towel

For a bath towel, you will need designs A, E, D, and C in that order, applied above border of towel.

Repeat steps 2, 3 under pillowcase.

Cut out patterns for required number of designs; repeat steps 5, 6, 7 under pillowcase to finish.

Hand towel

For a hand towel, you'll need three designs: A, D, and B to be applied in that order above border.

Repeat steps 2, 3 under pillowcase.

Cut out the three patterns, keeping them in order. Repeat steps 5, 6, 7 under pillowcase.

Washcloth

For a washcloth you will need one design; Design E. This design is put just above border on cloth.

Repeat steps 2, 3 under pillowcase.

Cut out applique pattern for the design. Then, repeat steps 5, 6, and 7 given under pillowcase.

DESIGN A

DESIGN B

DESIGN C

DESIGN D

DESIGN E

ACTUAL SIZE

DESIGN F

SUNNY STITCHING

Yellow sunning mat, page 34. You'll need 2½ yards yellow canvas, 31 inches wide and 1/6 yard scraps in contrasting color for the applique; 2 yards 6″-deep cotton fringe. If canvas does not have selvage edges, you'll need 6 yards bias tape matching canvas color for binding cut edges.

If canvas has no selvages, machine-sew bias tape along two edges. Draw 12″ circle on paper and add nine 4½″-long rays around the diameter. Cut out rays for pattern. Cut rays from contrasting canvas. No seam allowance is needed. Pin on mat; baste. Machine-sew rays using satin stitch. Cut fringe allowing 1″ at each end to turn under. Sew to mat twice across by machine.

Child's sunning mat, page 34. You'll need a 22″x45″ piece of dark blue canvas, ¼ yard red canvas, scrap of yellow canvas, 2½ yards bias tape, 1⅓ yards 4″-deep fringe. Cut bias tape and bind raw sides of mat. Draw pattern for 11½″x6″ lobster body and separate pieces for jointed legs. Cut red canvas pieces from pattern (no seam allowance) and pin in place 6″ from bottom of mat. Baste. Sew to mat with satin stitch, set at widest. Cut fringe, allowing 1″ to turn under at four ends. Machine-sew to mat twice across.

Leaf design drum pillow, page 34. You'll need pillow form 13″ diameter, 2″ deep, two 14″x14″ squares light green canvas, a 13″x 14″ strip white canvas, a 13″x13″ square of yellow canvas for applique. Cut two 14″ diameter circles from green canvas. Cut applique pattern from leaf drawn 11½″ long.

Cut out from yellow canvas. Pin on a green square; baste. Machine-stitch around design using satin stitch full width. Allowing 1″ seam, join 3″ ends white canvas. With right sides together, wrong sides out, sew white canvas to green appliqued circle. With right sides together, sew other edge of white strip to second green circle, leaving opening for insertion of pillow. Turn cover, insert pillow. Slip-stitch opening by hand.

Sun design flat pillow, page 34. You'll need flat pillow form, two squares yellow canvas 18″x18″, a 14″ square orange canvas for applique design, 1⅝ yards yellow bias tape. Cut two circles from 18″ canvas pieces.

Draw sun circle pattern with 8½″ diameter center and eleven 3″-long rays surrounding it. Cut sun's center, rays separately from orange canvas. Baste applique pieces to yellow circle letting center circle just meet inner rims of rays. With orange thread, machine-stitch center and inner bases of rays at same time with one row satin stitching.

Stitch outer edges of rays. Place yellow circles together, wrong sides together, and machine-stitch one-half way around. Add pillow form; continue sewing around. Topstitch bias tape to bind the seam.

Melon design pillow, page 34. You'll need pillow form 15″ square, one piece blue canvas 16″x16″, one piece chartreuse canvas 16″ x16″, red canvas 7″x10″, scraps of black and chartreuse canvas. Draw pattern for watermelon slice 11″ wide, 7½″ deep. Inner edge of rind is 10″ across, 6½″ deep. Add seven oval seeds to pattern. Cut pattern parts separately. Cut out rind from chartreuse scrap, melon from red, seeds from black, and baste on blue canvas square. Rind should just meet red melon edge. With dark green thread and satin stitch, machine-stitch outer rind and with white thread and satin stitch sew rind and melon on at same time. Sew top edge of melon with red thread. Sew each seed with black thread—all with satin stitch. Sew on chartreuse pillow back, adding pillow form. Whipstitch the opening closed by hand.

Orange design pillow, page 34. You'll need a 13″ square pillow form, two pieces yellow canvas 14″x14″, a 10″ square white canvas, a 10″ square orange canvas. Draw 9″ circle pattern for outside of design. Draw 8½″ circle and divide into seven sections leaving roughly a half inch between each. Pin 9″ pattern on white canvas and cut. Cut sections of orange canvas, pin on white circle. Applique sections to white circle using a satin stitch full width, orange thread. Sew orange design to one yellow piece with satin stitch.

Right sides together, sew three sides of two yellow pieces together. Turn. Insert pillow. Whipstitch the last side by hand.

Square sun design pillow, page 34. You'll need a pillow form 15″ square, a 16″x16″ section of orange canvas, 16″x16″ square yellow canvas, 10″x10″ square white canvas, one 10″x10″ square yellow canvas. Cut 8″ circle from yellow 10″ square. Cut eight 3″ long rays from white canvas. Arrange rays, yellow circle on orange canvas in sun shape—rays just meet circle edge. Using yellow thread, sew on (satin stitch) circle, inner bases of rays. Use white thread to sew on edges of rays. Sew yellow backing to orange top, leaving one side open. Insert pillow and whipstitch last side by hand.

Patio tablecloth, page 34. You'll need $3\frac{1}{2}$ yards of canvas for a standard-size picnic table, plus canvas for appliques in two colors (white and chartreuse flowers on a blue background were used for photo), bias tape matching base cloth. Cut two pieces of base cloth canvas that are 46″x31″. Cut two pieces base cloth canvas that are $10\frac{1}{2}$″x$25\frac{1}{4}$″.

Take one larger piece, one smaller piece; center lengthwise side of smaller to lengthwise side of larger; join together with regular machine stitch. Repeat with other set. (Two lengths of fabric are used to go across table. Flap is attached to one ,end of each to hang over narrow ends of table.)

Bind all outer edges with bias tape, using regular machine stitch. Draw the flower shapes on paper, varying sizes from 8″ to 3″. Cut out seventeen flowers of the various sizes from contrasting colors of canvas. Put flowers on cloth, arranging until you find design that pleases you. Baste in place.

Machine-stitch flowers with satin stitch full width. Press the finished cloth.

Design for swinging chair, page 34. You will need a solid colored canvas cover for swinging circle chair, or you may make one, using old cover as pattern. In addition, you will need canvas for applique in assorted colors (photo shows yellow flower center and white petals, moss green stem, a green leaf, a moss green leaf, and a brown root.)

Make patterns for designs. Circle for center is $3\frac{1}{2}$″ in diameter. Leaves measure 4″ long, $2\frac{1}{2}$″ side at widest parts. Petals should be a $5\frac{1}{2}$″-diameter circle with nine scallops around circumference. Stem is 8″ long; it measures $1\frac{1}{2}$″ wide at base and tapers to $\frac{1}{2}$″ at top. Roots have six divisions; they are approximately $11\frac{1}{2}$″ long overall and spread to $10\frac{1}{2}$″ width at base and 2″ at top. Cut out pieces. Position pattern in center of top half circle of chair canvas, base of stem at center seam line. Mark with pins.

Replace pattern pieces with canvas pieces. Baste into place with a middle width zigzag stitch. With thread matching each piece of applique, machine-stitch using satin stitch full width. Be sure to let flower petals cover stem top, stem cover the tops of roots.

Umbrella cover, page 34. You'll need a ready-made canvas cover in solid color, or make cover, using old cover as pattern. For applique design, you'll need a 13″ square of vinyl or acrylic coated canvas. Most umbrellas would require six of these for positioning of one flower per space between spokes. In addition, plan on using water-base glue.

Cut a 5-petaled $12\frac{1}{2}$″ in diameter flower pattern. Pin on canvas square and cut. Repeat for each flower until you have enough to position one flower between each set of spokes. Paint water base glue on the back side of one of the applique pieces. Apply to canvas and hold in position until it is dry (or place weights on applique to keep it flat while it's drying.) Position next applique and glue, continuing this process until all of the flowers are in place.

SUNNY STITCHING

Bird and nest design, circle chair, page 35. You'll need a ready-made canvas cover for a circle chair, or use an old cover as a pattern for new one. In addition, you'll need canvas in assorted colors for applique. Photo shows turquoise bird; blue eye; chartreuse beak; tail feathers of green, blue, purple; brown nest; turquoise eggs. A 10x15″ piece of canvas is needed for body.

Make paper pattern with bird's body 13″ long and 8½″ deep. Draw on five tail feathers, a scalloped wing, eye, beak, legs. Add nest made of branch shapes interlocked and measuring about 17″ wide. Draw five 3″-long eggs. Now draw separate pattern pieces using your first drawing as a guide. Pin first pattern on center top half of cover; legs of bird should just meet center seam. Cut out pieces from canvas. Replace paper pattern with canvas pieces. Baste with middle width zigzag stitch. Machine-stitch with a satin stitch. Center paper pattern for nest and eggs on lower half canvas cover, just meeting bird's legs. Cut canvas. Baste on. Stitch with satin stitch full width.

Butterfly chair, page 35. You'll need a solid canvas cover for butterfly chair, or if making your own cover, buy matching wide bias tape and cotton twill tape to reinforce center seam. If making cover, take old cover apart for a pattern. Allow a piece of canvas to reinforce corners. Apply applique before joining top and bottom pieces. Join with French seam and bind seam with cotton twill. Use bias tape to bind edges of the cover.

To applique ready-made cover, draw free-form designs, one for top half, one for bottom half. Both will be cut on fold, so you need only half a design. Top design should measure approximately 18″ at the fold and be 15″ across (for half of design). Chair seat design should be 15½″ on fold line and measure 13½″ across (for half of design).

Pin patterns on neatly folded canvas and draw around design with pencil to facilitate cutting intricate shapes. Cut. Unfold the canvas and pin on chair top and seat. Machine baste, using middle width loose zigzag stitch. Machine sew using full width of the satin stitch. Press the appliques.

Flower design circle chair, page 35. You'll need ready-made canvas cover for a circle chair, or use an old cover as a pattern for a new one. For applique, you'll need canvas in assorted colors. Photo shows an orange flower center, red petals, moss green stem and roots, one chartreuse leaf, one leaf of medium green. Draw pattern on paper first. Flower center is 6½″ circle; petals are cut from 8½″ circle (10 petals); two leaves are 5″ long each; stem is 6″ long and measures 3″ at base; divided roots are approximately 10½″ long, they spread from 3″ at top to 10½″ at the base. Cut canvas for each piece.

Baste applique pieces in place using middle zigzag stitch on machine. Machine-stitch using full width satin stitch, with thread matching each applique piece. Roots go on chair seat, flower goes on chair top.

Sun seats, page 35. You'll need fabric strips, any desired length, preferably leftover canvas. In addition, buy bias tape that matches. Cut strips 10″ wide, taper one end to a point. Baste bias tape to bind the raw edges. Sew the tape by machine using satin stitch or by hand with back stitch.

Mushroom design director's chair, page 35. You'll need canvas for seat and back—½ yard of 50″ fabric or ⅔ yard of 30″ fabric; scraps of assorted colors of canvas for appliqueing (photo shows bright blue, medium blue, moss green, blue-green, and chartreuse used on orange); two pieces of dowel 16″ long and ¼″ in diameter to hold seat canvas in side grooves.

For seat and back, measure and cut canvas using old seat cover as a pattern. Do not make seams until applique is done. Draw seven mushroom shapes varying in height from 4¾″ to 10½″. Cut stems and tops separately

Cut canvas for seat cover and reinforcement, allowing ample fabric for turning under at ends. Draw paper pattern of 11″ circle, separated into six angular spokes. Cut design from canvas and applique on seat using satin stitch full width.

Join the seat cover and reinforcement with hem along the long edges. Turn under the ends and tack in place.

Flower design pillow, page 35. You'll need a pillow form 12″ square, 2″ deep; two squares red canvas 13x13″ each; one strip white canvas 53x3″, one square white canvas 10x10″. Draw pattern of 5-petaled flower approximately 10″ across. Cut from white canvas square, pin and baste on red square, machine-stitch with satin stitch full width.

Join appliqued piece to white strip, then join to second red square, sewing halfway only. Insert pillow, whipstitch opening by hand.

Lemon design pillow, page 35. You'll need a pillow form 12″ square, 2″ deep; two 13x 13″ pieces chartreuse canvas; 1 strip dark green canvas 15x3″; 10″ squares of both yellow and white canvas. Cut 9½″ circle from white canvas, pin on chartreuse square. With yellow thread, satin-stitch white circle to square. Cut 6 sections yellow canvas from a circle about 9″ in diameter. Pin on white appliqued circle; sew using satin stitch.

Join appliqued square to dark green strip; then to second chartreuse square leaving an opening for pillow. Finish by hand.

Floral design director's chair, page 35. You'll need canvas seat and back for a director's chair, canvas for applique in many colors (photo shows light green stems and flowers of yellow, orange, blue, and red on a white background). Draw pattern for four simple flower shapes 5½″ long. Draw one flower for seat 13″ long. Pin patterns on canvas scraps, cut. Position four smaller flowers on the canvas back. Do not allow designs to overlap side seams of back. Pin. Baste. Do the same positioning, pinning, basting for larger flower on seat. With thread matching each piece of applique, machine-stitch, using satin stitch full width. (For best effect, make flowers of different types—one a daisy, one a tulip, a rose, a buttercup.)

when you cut out pattern. Cut designs from canvas scraps; pin six to chair back and one to chair seat. Baste with mushroom tops overlapping stems. Machine-stitch with satin stitch set at full width. Hem and edge back and seat. Insert dowels.

Apple design director's chair, page 35. You'll need ready-made cover for director's chair, or make your own of canvas using the old cover as pattern; scraps of assorted colors of canvas (photo shows red, white, blue, and green used on yellow). Draw patterns on paper of three 4½″ apples and one 3″ apple, leaves. Draw cross-section in one large apple (this will be cut from white). Cut from canvas scraps, position three apples on the chair's back, small apple on chair seat and baste. Machine-stitch using satin stitch at full width —use thread matching applique for the best-looking finished results.

Three-leaf design pillow, page 35. You'll need pillow form 13″ diameter, 2″ deep; two squares 14″x14″ chartreuse canvas, 1 strip yellow canvas 3″x44″, yellow canvas scraps.

Cut two circles 14″ in diameters from the chartreuse 14″ canvas squares. Draw pattern for three 5½″-long leaves. Cut from yellow canvas scraps. Pin leaves on one chartreuse square, baste. Machine-stitch, using satin stitch full width. Allowing 1″ seam, join 3″ ends of yellow canvas strip. With right sides together, sew strip to chartreuse appliqued circle. Sew other edge of strip to half of second green circle. Turn right side out and insert pillow. Whipstitch opening by hand.

Spoke design on folding stool, page 35. You'll need canvas for seat—about 15″ (use old seat as pattern) plus second layer of canvas to reinforce seat; canvas for applique design (photo shows yellow); upholstery tacks.

1. Teneriffe border for blouse

Materials needed:
1 ball pearl cotton in Myrtle
1 No. 20 tapestry needle

Directions: Make each border ½ inch out from front band of the blouse, as in photo on page 36.

Diagram below shows set of three motifs from A to B. For border, repeat from A to B as many times as you need.

Trace pattern; transfer dots from tracing onto stiff paper or onto a lightweight cardboard.

Then, pierce each dot with tip of tapestry needle. Indicate dots with a pencil on blouse. Do keep motifs straight.

With long and straight stitches, make an 8-stitch web radiating from center as indicated.

Weave over web on right side only; bring the weaving threads close together.

Starting at any stitch at center on first motif, weave in and out over the 8-stitch web to within the dotted line. Work other motifs same way. Make zigzag line around each border in straight stitches.

2. Teneriffe ring shown on girl's dress

Materials needed:
1 ball pearl cotton in Canary Yellow
1 No. 20 tapestry needle

Directions: Place a pin on yoke to indicate center of motif. Transfer dots from tracing of diagram onto a stiff paper, then pierce each dot with tip of tapestry needle. Matching center dot of diagram with pin, place pierced paper on yoke. Indicate dots with pencil on yoke for webs of motif.

With long and straight stitches make an 8-stitch web radiating from the center; then make two ¼ inch straight stitches between each long straight stitch of the 8-stitch web for the outer web. See indication on the diagram.

Weave over webs on the right side only; bring the weaving threads close together. Starting at any stitch at center, weave as shown over center web to within the first dotted line. Then work over the 3-stitch web from second dotted line to within the third dotted line. Following the heavy lines on the diagram, work first the outer zigzag line, then work the V stitches between inner and outer webs. Repeat for each ring.

3. Crewel flowers

Materials needed: Six-strand embroidery floss, 1 skein each of Chartreuse, Dk. Oriental Blue, Purple, Royal Purple, Violet, Dk. Willow Green, Leaf Green, and you'll need a No. 7 embroidery needle.

Directions: Trace design and transfer to fabric. Use three-strand floss for all work; follow diagram and color key for stitches and colors.

Flowers make perfect designs for crewel embroidery. You can make the individual designs smaller or add more if you wish—of course, you can change the colors, too. Be sure to select related colors for flowers.

4. Crewel leaves, stem

Materials needed: Six-strand embroidery floss, 1 skein each of Mid Pink, Myrtle, Jewel Rose, and No. 7 embroidery needle.

Directions: Transfer design to fabric. Use three strands of floss to work.

5. Crewel squirrel

Materials needed: Six-strand embroidery floss, 1 skein each of Dk. Orange, Dk. Yellow, Tropic Orange, ½ yard of Black, and No. 7 embroidery needle.

Directions: Transfer design to fabric. Use three strands of floss to work.

CREWEL AND TENERIFFE

Key for Stitches and Colors 3

- ꜱ Stem—Dk. Willow Green
- ꜱ Stem—Leaf Green
- ꜱ Stem—Chartreuse
- ꙮ Chain—Violet
- ШШ Buttonhole—Dk. Willow Green
- ✳ Seeding—Dk. Willow Green
- ꝏ Seeding—Chartreuse
- ꙮ Rumanian—Royal Purple
- ⊞ Satin—Royal Purple
- ⁛ Satin—Chartreuse
- ● Satin—Violet
- ▽ Satin—Purple
- ≋ Satin—Oriental Blue
- ◇ Satin—Dk. Willow Green
- • French Knot—Oriental Blue
- ◉ French Knot—Chartreuse
- ✕ French Knot—Violet

Key for Stitches and Colors 4

- ꜱ Stem—Myrtle
- ⫽ Satin—Myrtle
- ● Satin—Mid Pink
- ⊠ Satin—Jewel Rose
- ◉ French Knot—Jewel Rose
- • French Knot—Myrtle

Key for Stitches and Colors 5

- ╱ Stem—Tropic Orange
- ⸫ Stem—Dk. Yellow
- ╱ Stem—Dk. Orange
- ✕ Short and Long—Tropic Orange
- ‡ Satin—Tropic Orange
- ˅ Satin—Dk. Orange
- ♦ Satin—Black

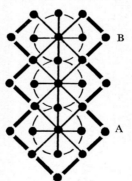

3

4

5

Stem and Crewel Stitch is illustrated in figure A above. Stem stitches are used to define the lines, or in parallel rows to fill an area. Anchor the thread so as to work away from you. Continue stitch until line or area is filled.

Short and Long stitches are illustrated in figure B, left.

The first row of the stitches is made of one short and of one long stitch that are worked alternately. The following rows are worked in stitches all the same length. This is a form of Satin Stitch that is used for shading and texture. The length of the stitch is adjusted to fit the outside contour of design.

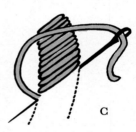

Satin Stitch is shown in figure C, left. Keep the straight stitches close together to fill in design.

This stitch is probably the best known of "filling" stitches used to cover large areas in a hurry. The thread is carried across an area in parallel stitches, returning underneath the fabric.

Be sure that the needle is slightly more slanted in the return stitch.

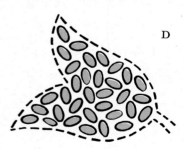

Seeding, illustrated in figure D, is a simple filling stitch that is composed of small Straight Stitches of equal size which are placed at random over the surface of the design as shown above.

Use this stitch for light filling of large areas such as flowers or leaves where a solid effect is not needed.

It takes some practice to make this stitch even. Try on a sample fabric.

A Stem and Crewel Stitch
B Short and Long Stitches
C Satin Stitch
D Seeding
E Rumanian Stitch
F Straight Stitch

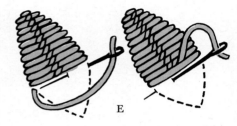

The Rumanian Stitch is shown in figure E above. This stitch is usually put to work filling a leaf or flower. It's worked from the top to bottom. Bring the thread through at the top left of the shape; carry the thread across and take a stitch on the right side of the shape with the thread below the needle (A). Take a stitch at left side, thread above needle (B).

These two movements are worked until the shape is filled. Keep the stitches close together for the best, finished look. The size of the center crossing stitch can be varied, either to make a longer oblique stitch or a small stitch that is straight. By varying the size of the center crossing stitch, you can actually alter the appearance of design itself. It's well to practice this on a sample piece of fabric before proceeding.

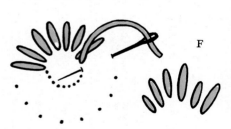

The Straight Stitch is illustrated in figure F above. This is shown as single-spaced stitches worked either in a regular or irregular manner. Sometimes these stitches are of varying size. The stitches should be neither too long nor too loose. The Straight Stitch is ideal for use as flower outlines, other simple design effects on wall hangings, samplers. It is one of the easiest stitches to master.

EMBROIDERY

How to transfer designs to fabric

To transfer the design to fabric, use carbon paper or trace the outline of the design with pencil. Place the paper on carbon side of paper and go over lines once more, thus transferring carbon to back of tracing. Anchor tracing (with carbon side down) in place. Press with a hot iron, being careful not to scorch fabric.

A smooth, padded surface should be used—preferably your ironing board, as bumps or depressions will prevent the outlines from marking properly.

Another way to transfer the design to the fabric is to trace the design on thin tracing or tissue paper with a 2H pencil; turn the penciled drawing face down on the cloth. Drip a puddle of ordinary lighter fluid on the back. While it is wet, rub all over it hard with the edge of a spoon. (Caution: Use a small amount at a time. Avoid inhaling fumes. Do not use under dry, cold conditions where static electricity might cause a spark.)

Several impressions can usually be made from a single drawing before it must be re-penciled. If you wish to reverse the design, simply trace pencil lines on other side of tracing and proceed as before. If penciled impressions are a little light, reinforce lines with a ballpoint pen; the ink does not run or smear on cloth.

On the following page are complete instructions for doing all the embroidery stitches needed to make the designs shown earlier, and to create your own designs.

French Knot Stitch

Bring needle up through fabric; hold tip of needle close to this point. Wrap thread over it one or more times, depending upon the size of dot. Hold thread taut by placing your thumb at "X" position. Swing needle in direction of arrow. Push it down through dot where first stitch was taken. Pull needle and thread through to back side, forming knot.

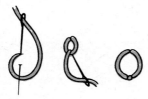

Lazy-Daisy Stitch

Make versatile stitch shown above similar to the Chain Stitch illustrated in the next column, but after each loop is completed, make a small stitch to secure it neatly in its place.

Make all Lazy-Daisy Stitches the same length, but vary the center securing stitch to any length desired to achieve different effects. Vary the outside stitches as much as necessary, also, as suggested in the drawing above.

Blanket Stitch

Insert needle up through the fabric, going under the upper thread forming a loop. Continue making over and under stitches as long as necessary and in any direction.

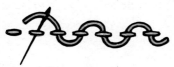

Running Stitch With Scallops

In this easy-to-do stitch you simply push the needle to the fabric surface from the back side. Push the needle below again as indicated in the drawing above. Continue making in and out stitches as needed. To add the scallops, thread needle through yarn stitch from one side, then through next stitch from other side, leaving yarn loose in scallops.

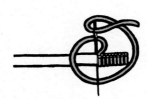

Buttonhole Stitch

Make a Running Stitch along line to be buttonholed. Then overcast along the line, working from right to left, as indicated in the drawing above. Use Buttonhole Stitch as a decorative accent or to applique fabric.

Cretan Stitch

To start stitch, pull thread through fabric near top. Starting point will mark beginning of row of stitches. Carry thread around to front and pass needle under a few threads of fabric on a horizontal line in a little below starting point. Needle will be turned toward center, carried

across slack thread. Make similar stitch on left side of start, with needle point back to right as shown above.

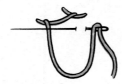

Third Cretan Stitch is on right side of center. Needle must be drawn across slack thread each time to produce desired twisted effect.

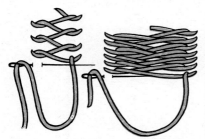

When working from top to bottom (you can work side-to-side) each stitch must be taken somewhat below one just made on other side of center line, rather than opposite it.

The basic Cretan Stitch is varied by changing the length of stitches on each side of center line, and/or the width between.

Chain Stitch

To make Chain Stitch, bring needle with thread to front side of fabric, hold thread to form loop. Needle should enter fabric where thread of previous stitch came through, then go over thread loop to complete stitch.

Plus-Time or Algerian Eye Stitch

Each star or eye consists of eight stitches that are all taken into a central point. Arrange the stitches in a square. For variation, use one color of the thread for the plus lines, another color of thread for the times lines.

Couching Stitch

Use Couching Stitch as an outline stitch or to secure other threads. Lay heavy thread to be couched on top of the fabric, shaping it to follow the design line. Pin the yarn in place to secure it before you start Couching Stitches.

If yarn is not too heavy, thread the needle and pull it through fabric to anchor the one end. Pull the needle holding finer yarn through the burlap close to the couching yarn.

Next, make a series of vertical stitches over the couching thread and through fabric to the back side. In order to make the stitches vertical on the front side of fabric, the needle must go through to the back side of the fabric in a diagonal direction. The stitch may be performed from the right to left as illustrated, from the left to the right, or up and down.

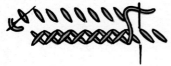

Cross Stitch

The Cross Stitch can be started either at the right or the left of the area to be decorated. To begin, make a row of slanted stitches of equal length and evenly spaced. Then, work back over them in the same direction. This makes a row of Cross Stitches. The reverse side will show a row of upright stitches.

Feather Stitch

With the thread under a slanted needle, make a Blanket Stitch to the right of a straight perpendicular line. With the thread under the needle, make a Blanket Stitch to the left. Repeat. Fancy Feather Stitch is made by working several stitches on each side. They may be evenly spaced or grouped. A further variation is made by pointing the needle straight down so the outside stitches are parallel and closed.

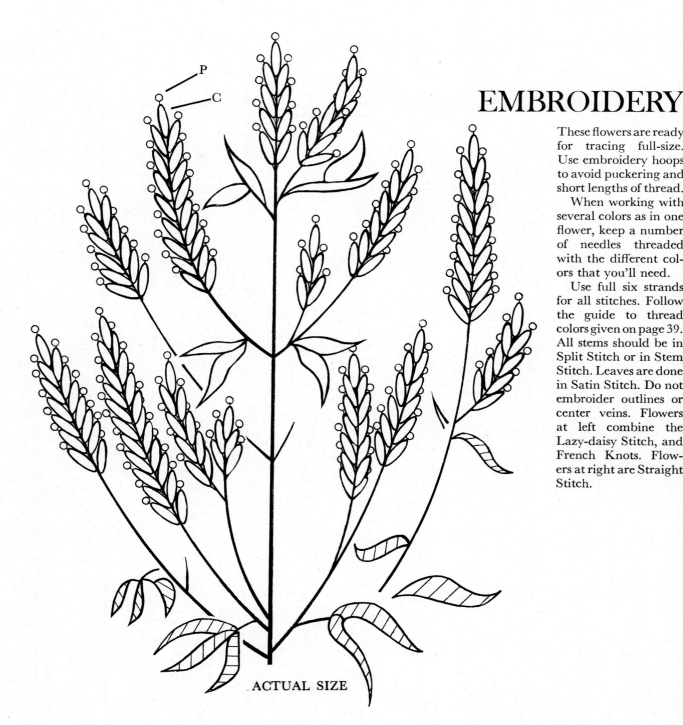

EMBROIDERY

These flowers are ready for tracing full-size. Use embroidery hoops to avoid puckering and short lengths of thread.

When working with several colors as in one flower, keep a number of needles threaded with the different colors that you'll need.

Use full six strands for all stitches. Follow the guide to thread colors given on page 39. All stems should be in Split Stitch or in Stem Stitch. Leaves are done in Satin Stitch. Do not embroider outlines or center veins. Flowers at left combine the Lazy-daisy Stitch, and French Knots. Flowers at right are Straight Stitch.

ACTUAL SIZE

ACTUAL SIZE

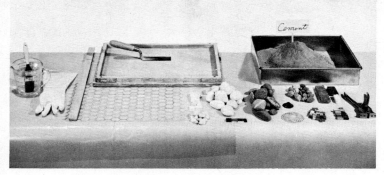

Pebbles, ready-mixed cement, and a little labor produce pebble mosaics. For the 3x5-foot garden wall, shown on page 69, make wood frame that measures 12x18x¾ inches. Join edges with angle irons. Frame sits, unattached on 13x19x¼-inch base.

MOSAICS

To prepare worktable, lay a sheet of clear plastic under mold to catch leftover cement, and keep area clean. Using small, stiff brush, saturate inner wood areas with water. Dampen corners.

Have pebbles sorted as to size, shape, color. Square-foot coverage, mixing directions are on package of the prepared cement; follow them carefully, using clean pan. Mix thoroughly.

Trowel base layer of cement ¼-inch deep, into mold, a bit at a time. Use pressure to make smooth and solid. Fill corners so pieces fit together evenly in final assembly. Level with trowel.

With tin snips, cut wire mesh to exact inner measure of the mold. Hold firmly with both hands; lay mesh evenly to front side of mold; drop it on cement. With glove, press it into cement until anchored.

Add layer of cement until even with frame top. Press, work in place. Finish coat secures mesh, holds pebbles. By working cement, bubbles are released, finish smooth.

Put flat piece of wood stripping (about 4 inches longer than frame) at front of filled mold. Hold ends with both hands; work rhythmically from side to side, toward you.

Hold pan securely between body and mold to catch excess cement. Empty drippings into paper. Wipe pan out well before the cement hardens in it. Wash pan.

Use pebbles from beach or yard. Gravel firms also have a wide choice. Cut piece of paper same size as the inner mold. Lay design on paper. Pebble shapes suggest ideas.

Transfer design from paper, moving one pebble at a time. Lay pebble in place in cement; anchor it by holding firmly and wiggling it into position. Plan design on total area to be covered.

Using trowel handle or small rubber mallet, pound each pebble deep enough into cement to hold it firm. Pebbles don't have to be even. You may wish some high and low to give depth.

Allow your mosaic to set for at least 24 hours, then hold it upright. Tap the frame gently around the edges. Repeat tapping on edge of the base to release cement. When all panels needed to complete the project (in this case, the garden wall) have been made, you can apply waterproof tile mastic to the back of the mosaic and to the area to be covered. When the mastic is tacky, put your mosaic in position. Project will add a decorative note to your garden.

1. This idea lets you display children's art in a bright frame and change pictures in seconds. Spray a cookie sheet with spray enamel. Fasten artwork on with small magnets. Drill a hole in tray or solder on a small loop of wire for hanging your picture.

2. Family photos displayed this way make a colorful wall hanging. Get favorite snapshots enlarged to 5x7 inches. Buy inexpensive wood or metal frames; spray-enamel them in bright colors. Paint rectangle of ½-inch plywood. Mount framed snapshots with brads or glue.

3. To make this frame, outline print on ½-inch plywood, leaving a 3-inch border all around. Lay masking tape on inside of print outline, then smooth a layer of thinly mixed water base wood putty on border. Use a comb to make textured effect in putty before it dries. When dry, remove tape, mount print. Finish with painted wood strips nailed around outer edge of plywood and bordering print.

4. Mount poster on piece of hardboard; glue insulation cork to plywood backing. Glue the mounted poster to cork, or "float" it off background by gluing two strips of wood to cork and poster to the woodstrips.

5. Trace around Christmas cards on hardboard, then cut out hardboard about ⅛-inch outside outline. Round off edge with sandpaper and spray edges with gold paint. Glue cards to hardboard pieces. Spray frame gold, cut hardboard piece to fit frame. Glue felt to piece, fasten in frame. Glue cards to felt.

6. Cut backing piece of hardboard or illustration board to size of poster. Nail ¾x¾-inch wood frame to back of backing piece, flush with edges. Glue poster to front of the backing piece. Stain pieces of wood lath, nail around edges, nailing into frame on backing piece. Make plain butt joints at corners.

7. Glue print to hardboard backing, then cut ½-inch piece of plywood about 6 inches larger than print. Pad 3-inch border with strips of paper or packing material, then put leather-patterned vinyl over padding and tack or staple to plywood. Lay print in place and fasten to plywood with row of decorative upholstery tacks. Drive tacks into plywood, letting the heads overlap edge of print backing. Put another row around outside edge of plywood.

8. For a primitive or Early American print, mount it on a hardboard backing, then cut weathered boards to roughly same length and fasten them together with wood strips nailed across back. Glue print to the boards.

9. To make this frame, nail wood strips to piece of backing (see instructions for 6), then glue print to backing. Glue strips of wood edging tape along edges of picture. Cut the miters at the corners with scissors or a sharp knife. Put tape on edges, too, to cover strips on back of print. Stain or oil the wood tape with a small brush.

10. Group pictures from a book on a fabric background. Cover a piece of hardboard with fabric, glue on, then glue clipped-out pictures to fabric. We added border of gold deckle. Cover with a matching-size piece of glass and hold it all together with plastic hanger-clamps—get them at a framing shop.

PICTURE FRAMES

INDEX